EMBRACING NEURODIVERSITY

UNDERSTANDING AND THRIVING WITH YOUR UNIQUE BRAIN

PSYCHOLOGY THAT HELPS YOU

LEE HOPKINS

WITH

CLAUDE LECLERQUE

°138

Published by degrees138, Adelaide, South Australia—degrees138.com

Dedicated to everyone who wonders if I am writing about them.

I am.

"I love deadlines. I like the whooshing sound they make as they fly by."

DOUGLAS ADAMS

CHAPTER 1
THE NEURODIVERSITY SPECTRUM

IMAGINE, if you will, a world where everyone's brain worked in exactly the same way. How dreadfully dull that would be! Fortunately, we live in a far more interesting reality, one where the human brain comes in a delightful array of flavours, each with its own unique blend of strengths, challenges, and quirks. Welcome to the wonderfully colourful world of neurodiversity.

The term 'neurodiversity' was coined in the late 1990s by Australian sociologist Judy Singer, who herself is on the autism spectrum. It's a concept that acknowledges and celebrates the natural variation in human brain function and behaviour. Rather than viewing these differences as disorders or deficits, neurodiversity recognises them as valuable aspects of human diversity.

THE NEURODIVERSITY PARADIGM

Before we dive into the specific conditions that fall under the neurodiversity umbrella, it's worth taking a moment to explore the neurodiversity paradigm itself. This perspective challenges the traditional medical model of mental functioning, which tends to pathologise brain differences.

The neurodiversity paradigm posits that:

1. Neurological differences are natural variations in the human genome, much like biodiversity in an ecosystem.

2. These differences are not inherently good or bad, they're simply different.

3. The challenges faced by neurodivergent individuals are often the result of a mismatch between their neurotype and the environment, rather than a problem with the individual themselves.

4. Society benefits from the inclusion and contributions of neurodivergent individuals.

This shift in perspective has profound implications for how we understand and support neurodivergent individuals. Rather than focusing solely on 'fixing' or 'curing' neurodevelopmental conditions, the neurodiversity movement advocates for acceptance, accommodation, and celebration of neurological differences.

Now, let's embark on a whistle-stop tour of some common neurodevelopmental conditions that fall under the neurodiversity umbrella. Buckle up, dear reader, for we're about to traverse the fascinating landscape of the human mind.

AUTISM SPECTRUM DISORDER (ASD)

First stop on our neurodiversity journey is Autism. If the human brain were a computer, those with autism might be running a different operating system—not better or worse, mind you, simply different.

. . .

INDIVIDUALS WITH AUTISM OFTEN HAVE:

- Unique ways of perceiving and interacting with the world

- Intense focus on specific interests

- Challenges with social communication and interaction

- Sensory sensitivities (more on this later—it's not all bad news!)

Let's delve a bit deeper into each of these characteristics:

UNIQUE PERCEPTION AND INTERACTION

Individuals with autism often perceive the world in a markedly different way from neurotypical individuals. This can manifest in various ways:

- Attention to detail: Many autistic individuals have an exceptional ability to notice and remember small details that others might overlook. This can be a tremendous asset in fields requiring precision, such as quality control or scientific research.

- Literal thinking: Autistic individuals often interpret language literally, which can lead to misunderstandings but can also result in novel and insightful interpretations of information.

- Different sensory experiences: The world might look, sound, feel, smell, and taste different to an autistic person. This can be overwhelming at times but can also lead to unique artistic expressions or innovations in sensory-based fields.

Intense focus and special interests

One of the hallmarks of autism is the capacity for intense focus on specific topics or activities. This trait, often referred to as 'special interests', can lead to:

- Deep expertise: Autistic individuals often become veritable encyclopedias on their topics of interest, accumulating vast amounts of knowledge.

- Innovation: The ability to focus intensely on a subject can lead to novel insights and breakthroughs in various fields.

- Job skills: When special interests align with career paths, autistic individuals can become exceptionally skilled and dedicated professionals.

Social communication challenges

While social interaction can be challenging for many autistic individuals, it's important to note that autism doesn't equate to a lack of desire for social connection. Common social communication challenges include:

- Difficulty interpreting non-verbal cues: Body language, facial expressions, and tone of voice can be challenging to decode for many autistic individuals.

- Challenges with small talk: The art of casual conversation can be perplexing, as it often seems to lack a clear purpose or structure.

- Direct communication style: Many autistic individuals prefer clear, direct communication, which can sometimes be perceived as blunt by neurotypical standards.

SENSORY SENSITIVITIES

Sensory processing differences are a key aspect of autism. These can include:

- Hypersensitivity: Certain sensory inputs might be experienced as overwhelmingly intense. For example, a sound that's barely noticeable to others might be painfully loud to an autistic person.

- Hyposensitivity: Some sensory inputs might not register as strongly, leading to a need for more intense stimulation in certain areas.

- Sensory seeking: Some autistic individuals actively seek out certain sensory experiences, finding them calming or pleasurable.

It's crucial to remember that autism is a spectrum, and these traits can manifest in vastly different ways and intensities among individuals. No two autistic people are exactly alike, hence the saying, "If you've met one person with autism, you've met one person with autism."

For a comprehensive overview of autism, the Autism Awareness Australia website (https://www.autismawareness. com.au/) offers a wealth of information and resources.

ATTENTION DEFICIT HYPERACTIVITY DISORDER (ADHD)

Next up, we have ADHD. If the neurotypical brain is a well-behaved labrador, the ADHD brain is more akin to an excitable border collie—always on the go, easily distracted, but capable of intense focus when properly engaged.

Common traits of ADHD include:

- Difficulty maintaining attention

- Hyperactivity and impulsivity

- Challenges with organisation and time management

- Creative thinking and problem-solving skills

Let's explore each of these in more detail.

ATTENTION DIFFICULTIES

The 'attention deficit' part of ADHD is somewhat of a misnomer. Rather than a deficit of attention, individuals with ADHD often have difficulty regulating their attention. This can manifest as:

- Distractibility: People with ADHD might find their attention easily pulled away by external stimuli or internal thoughts.

- Hyperfocus: Conversely, when engaged in an interesting task, individuals with ADHD can enter a state of intense concentration, losing track of time and their surroundings.

- Inconsistent performance: Due to fluctuations in attention, performance in work or school can be inconsistent, leading to frustration and misunderstandings.

HYPERACTIVITY AND IMPULSIVITY

The 'hyperactive' aspect of ADHD can look different in different people and can change over the lifespan:

- Physical restlessness: This might manifest as fidgeting, pacing, or difficulty sitting still.

- Mental restlessness: Even when physically still, individuals with ADHD might experience racing thoughts or a constant need for mental stimulation.

- Impulsivity: Acting without fully considering the conse-quences is common, which can lead to both positive (spontaneity, quick decision-making) and negative (risk-taking behaviours) outcomes.

Executive Function Challenges

ADHD is fundamentally a disorder of executive function, which encompasses skills like organisation, time management, and emotional regulation:

- Difficulty with organisation: Keeping track of tasks, belongings, and commitments can be a significant challenge.

- Time blindness: Many individuals with ADHD struggle with estimating how long tasks will take and managing their time effectively.

- Emotional dysregulation: Intense emotions and difficulty regulating emotional responses are common in ADHD.

Creative Thinking and Problem-Solving

While ADHD presents many challenges, it also comes with significant strengths:

- Out-of-the-box thinking: The ADHD brain often makes unique connections, leading to creative solutions and innovative ideas.

- Adaptability: The ability to shift focus quickly can be an asset in fast-paced or changing environments.

- Enthusiasm and energy: When engaged in interesting tasks, individuals with ADHD can bring an infectious energy and passion to their work.

It's important to note that ADHD can present differently in different individuals. Traditionally, ADHD was divided into three subtypes: predominantly inattentive, predominantly hyperactive-impulsive, and combined type. However, current understanding recognises that these presentations can fluctuate over time and in different contexts.

For more information on ADHD, the Australian ADHD Professionals Association (https://aadpa.com.au/) provides evidence-based resources and support.

DYSLEXIA

Ah, dyslexia—the condition that turns the written word into a particularly frustrating game of Scrabble. Individuals with dyslexia often struggle with reading, writing, and spelling, but they also tend to be highly creative and excel at big-picture thinking.

Key features of dyslexia include:

- Difficulties with reading and spelling

- Challenges with phonological processing

- Strengths in visual-spatial reasoning

- Innovative thinking and problem-solving abilities

Let's unpack each of these aspects.

READING AND SPELLING DIFFICULTIES

The most well-known aspect of dyslexia is its impact on reading and spelling:

- Slow or inaccurate reading: Words might appear to move on the page, or letters might seem to jumble or reverse.

- Spelling inconsistencies: Even common words might be spelled differently each time they're written.

- Difficulty with unfamiliar words: Sounding out new words can be particularly challenging.

PHONOLOGICAL PROCESSING CHALLENGES

At its core, dyslexia involves difficulties with processing the sounds of language:

- Phonemic awareness: Identifying and manipulating individual sounds in words can be challenging.

- Rapid naming: Quickly naming familiar objects, colours, or letters might be difficult.

- Auditory processing: Following verbal instructions or remembering spoken information can be problematic.

VISUAL-SPATIAL STRENGTHS

Many individuals with dyslexia have strengths in visual-spatial reasoning:

- 3D thinking: Visualising objects in three dimensions and mentally rotating them can be a particular strength.

- Pattern recognition: Identifying patterns and connections in complex systems often comes naturally.

- Big picture thinking: While details might be challenging, understanding overarching concepts and systems is often a strength.

INNOVATIVE THINKING

The dyslexic brain often excels at thinking outside the box:

- Creative problem-solving: Approaching problems from unique angles can lead to innovative solutions.

- Entrepreneurial skills: Many successful entrepreneurs have dyslexia, possibly due to their ability to see opportunities others might miss.

- Interdisciplinary thinking: Making connections across different fields or subjects is often a strength.

It's worth noting that dyslexia exists on a spectrum, and its impact can vary significantly from person to person. Some individuals with dyslexia might struggle primarily with reading, while others might have more difficulty with writing or math (a related condition called dyscalculia).

The Australian Dyslexia Association (https://dyslexiaassocia tion.org.au/) offers comprehensive information and support for individuals with dyslexia.

TOURETTE SYNDROME

Tourette Syndrome, contrary to popular belief, is not simply about involuntary swearing (though that can be a part of it for some). It's characterised by repetitive, involuntary movements and vocalisations called tics.

Individuals with Tourette Syndrome may experience:

- Motor tics (e.g., blinking, shoulder shrugging)

- Vocal tics (e.g., throat clearing, repeating words)

- Heightened sensory awareness

- Impressive creative and musical abilities

Let's explore these aspects in more detail.

. . .

Motor tics

Motor tics are involuntary movements that can range from small, barely noticeable actions to larger, more obvious movements:

- Simple motor tics: These might include eye blinking, facial grimacing, head jerking, or shoulder shrugging.

- Complex motor tics: These involve more coordinated movements, such as touching objects, hopping, or performing a sequence of movements.

Vocal tics

Vocal tics involve sounds made through the nose, mouth, or throat:

- Simple vocal tics: These might include throat clearing, sniffing, or grunting.

- Complex vocal tics: These could involve saying words or phrases out of context. Coprolalia, the involuntary uttering of obscene words, is a complex vocal tic that affects only a small percentage of people with Tourette's.

Sensory experiences

Many individuals with Tourette Syndrome report heightened sensory awareness:

- Premonitory urges: Many people with Tourette's describe feeling a buildup of tension before a tic, which is relieved by performing the tic.

- Sensory sensitivities: Similar to individuals with autism, some people with Tourette's may be more sensitive to certain sensory inputs.

. . .

CREATIVE AND MUSICAL ABILITIES

Interestingly, many individuals with Tourette Syndrome display impressive creative and musical abilities:

- Musical talent: There seems to be a higher prevalence of musical ability among individuals with Tourette's, though the reasons for this are not fully understood.

- Creativity: Many people with Tourette's report having vivid imaginations and excel in creative pursuits.

It's important to note that Tourette Syndrome often co-occurs with other neurodevelopmental conditions, particularly ADHD and OCD. The tics associated with Tourette's can wax and wane over time, and many individuals find that their tics decrease in frequency and severity as they enter adulthood.

For more information on Tourette Syndrome, the Tourette Syndrome Association of Australia (https://tourette.org.au/) is an excellent resource.

OTHER LESS COMMON NEURODIVERGENT CONDITIONS

While we've covered some of the more well-known neurodivergent conditions, it's important to note that the neurodiversity spectrum is vast and varied. Other conditions that fall under this umbrella include:

DYSCALCULIA

Dyscalculia is a specific learning difficulty related to mathematics. Individuals with dyscalculia might struggle with:

- Understanding number concepts

- Performing basic arithmetic

- Estimating quantities

- Understanding time and money

However, people with dyscalculia often have strengths in other areas, such as verbal skills, creative thinking, and spatial reasoning.

DYSPRAXIA

Also known as Developmental Coordination Disorder (DCD), dyspraxia affects motor coordination. Individuals with dyspraxia might experience:

- Difficulties with fine motor skills (e.g., writing, using utensils)

- Challenges with gross motor skills (e.g., balance, coordination)

- Problems with spatial awareness

- Difficulties with planning and organising tasks

Despite these challenges, individuals with dyspraxia often have strengths in verbal skills, empathy, and creative thinking.

SYNAESTHESIA

Synaesthesia is a fascinating neurological trait where stimulation of one sensory or cognitive pathway leads to involuntary experiences in another pathway. For example:

- Seeing colours when hearing music

- Tasting flavours when reading words

- Feeling textures when looking at numbers

Synaesthesia is not typically considered a disorder, as it doesn't usually interfere with daily life and can even enhance cognitive abilities in certain areas.

THE INTERSECTIONALITY OF NEURODIVERGENCE

It's crucial to understand that neurodevelopmental conditions often overlap and interact. Many individuals may have traits of multiple conditions, a phenomenon known as neurodevelopmental intersectionality. For example:

- ADHD and Autism: These conditions frequently co-occur, with some researchers suggesting they might be different expressions of similar underlying neurological differences.

- Dyslexia and Dyscalculia: It's common for individuals to struggle with both reading and maths.

- Tourette Syndrome and OCD: These conditions often co-occur and share some neurological underpinnings.

This intersectionality highlights the importance of viewing neurodiversity as a spectrum rather than discrete categories. Each individual's neurological profile is unique, shaped by a complex interplay of genetics, environment, and personal experiences.

THE NEURODIVERSITY MOVEMENT

As we conclude our tour of the neurodiversity spectrum, it's worth discussing the broader societal implications of the neurodiversity paradigm. The neurodiversity movement, which has gained significant momentum in recent years, advocates for several key principles:

1. Acceptance: Neurodevelopmental differences should be accepted as a natural part of human diversity, not pathologised or stigmatised.

2. Accommodation: Society should adapt to accommodate different neurotypes, rather than expecting all individuals to conform to a narrow definition of 'normal'.

3. Strengths-based approach: Instead of focusing solely on challenges or deficits, we should recognise and cultivate the unique strengths associated with different neurotypes.

4. Self-advocacy: Neurodivergent individuals should have a voice in decisions that affect them, following the principle of "Nothing About Us Without Us".

5. Neurodiversity-affirming support: While the neurodiversity paradigm doesn't deny the very real challenges faced by neurodivergent individuals, it advocates for support that affirms and empowers rather than aims to 'normalise'.

The neurodiversity movement has had a significant impact on how we understand and support neurodivergent individuals. For example:

- In education, there's a growing emphasis on differentiated instruction and universal design for learning, which aim to accommodate diverse learning styles and needs.

- In the workplace, many companies are recognising the value of neurodivergent employees and implementing neurodiversity hiring programs.

- In healthcare, there's a shift towards more person-centred, strengths-based approaches to supporting neurodivergent individuals.

CHALLENGES AND CONTROVERSIES

It's important to note that the neurodiversity paradigm is not without its controversies. Some of the challenges and debates include:

- Balancing acceptance with support: How do we celebrate neurodiversity while still acknowledging and addressing the very real challenges faced by many neurodivergent individuals?

- Representation: The neurodiversity movement has been criticised for sometimes focusing more on 'high-functioning' individuals, potentially overlooking the needs of those with more significant support needs.

- Medical model vs. social model: There's ongoing debate about the extent to which neurodevelopmental conditions should be viewed through a medical lens versus a social or cultural lens.

- Research priorities: How should research funding be allocated between searching for 'cures' or treatments and developing better supports and accommodations?

These debates highlight the complexity of neurodiversity and the importance of nuanced, thoughtful approaches to supporting neurodivergent individuals.

CONCLUSION

As we conclude our exploration of the neurodiversity spectrum, it's crucial to remember that these labels are not destinies. They're simply ways of understanding and describing different patterns of brain function. Every individual, regardless of their neurotype, is unique.

The neurodiversity paradigm invites us to embrace a more inclusive understanding of what it means to be human. It challenges us to create a world that values and accommodates all types of minds, recognising that our differences are not just challenges to be overcome, but sources of innovation, creativity, and strength.

In the words of the inimitable Dr. Seuss, "Why fit in when you were born to stand out?" Neurodiversity reminds us that there's no one 'right' way for a brain to work. So whether your brain is more of a sporty hatchback or a luxurious limousine, embrace its unique features. After all, it's the variety that makes the journey of life so fascinating.

As we move forward, let's strive to create a world that not only accepts neurodiversity but celebrates it. A world where everyone has the opportunity to thrive, not in spite of their differences, but because of them. For in the grand tapestry of human cognition, it's the vibrant threads of neurodiversity that create the most beautiful and intricate patterns.

CHAPTER 2
RECOGNISING NEURODIVERGENT TRAITS—A FIELD GUIDE TO THE WILD WORLD OF THE HUMAN BRAIN

WELCOME BACK, intrepid explorers of the mind! In our last chapter, we took a whirlwind tour of the neurodiversity spectrum. Now, we're going to don our pith helmets, grab our metaphorical magnifying glasses, and embark on a safari through the lush jungle of neurodivergent traits. Don't forget to pack your sense of humour—we might need it to fend off any particularly prickly characteristics we encounter!

COMMON CHARACTERISTICS OF NEURODIVERGENT INDIVIDUALS

Before we dive into the specifics of each neurodevelopmental condition, let's take a moment to appreciate some of the overarching traits that many neurodivergent individuals share. Think of these as the 'greatest hits' of neurodiversity, if you will.

1. UNIQUE THINKING PATTERNS

If neurotypical thinking is a straight highway, neurodivergent thinking is more like a scenic route through the countryside, complete with unexpected detours, charming villages, and the occasional cow blocking the road. This different way of processing information can lead to:

- Creative problem-solving: When life gives you lemons, most people make lemonade. A neurodivergent person might make a lemon-powered battery, write a sonnet about the colour yellow, or start a lucrative import/export business specialising in citrus fruits.

- Outside-the-box ideas: Why think outside the box when you can reimagine the very concept of 'box-ness' itself?

- Unique perspectives: Ever wonder what the world looks like to a giraffe? A neurodivergent person might not only wonder but create an entire philosophical treatise on giraffe epistemology.

2. Sensory sensitivities

Many neurodivergent individuals experience the world in high definition, surround sound, and sometimes even smell-o-vision. This can manifest as:

- Heightened sensitivity to stimuli: That fluorescent light isn't just annoying; it's staging a one-bulb rave in your eyeballs.

- Sensory seeking behaviours: Some neurodivergent folks are sensory thrill-seekers, always on the lookout for the next big tactile adventure.

- Difficulty filtering sensory input: Imagine trying to have a conversation while simultaneously listening to death metal, smelling a fish market, and being tickled by feathers. Welcome to a typical Tuesday for some neurodivergent individuals.

3. Intense focus and special interests

When a neurodivergent person finds a topic interesting, they don't just dip their toes in the water—they do a cannonball into the deep end and set up permanent residence with the fish. This can lead to:

- Encyclopedic knowledge of niche subjects: Need to know the average rainfall in Uzbekistan during the Pleistocene epoch? There's probably a neurodivergent person with that information ready to go.

- Hyperfocus: When engaged in a favoured activity, time becomes a mere suggestion, much like speed limits on a German autobahn.

- Passion-driven motivation: If harnessed properly, this intense focus could probably power a small city.

4. Social communication differences

Social interaction for many neurodivergent individuals is like trying to play chess while everyone else is playing checkers—and no one told you the rules of either game.

- Direct communication style: Why use a hundred words when ten will do? Efficiency is key, even if it occasionally leads to raised eyebrows or dropped jaws.

- Difficulty with small talk: "Nice weather we're having" is met with a detailed analysis of global climate patterns. Oops.

- Unique sense of humour: Often dry, sometimes unintentionally hilarious, and occasionally so clever it flies over everyone's heads like a stealth bomber.

5. Executive Function challenges

Executive function is like the CEO of your brain. In neurodivergent individuals, this CEO might be more of an eccentric startup founder than a Fortune 500 executive.

- Time blindness: Time is a social construct, right? Try telling that to your boss when you're three hours late for work.

- Difficulty with organisation: "Organised chaos" is not just a phrase; it's a lifestyle.

- Emotional regulation challenges: Feelings aren't just felt; they're experienced in full surround sound, IMAX 3D glory.

Now that we've covered these overarching traits, let's dive into the specific characteristics of some common neurodevelopmental conditions. Remember, this isn't a diagnostic tool—it's more of a "friend finder" for your brain. If you find yourself nodding along and muttering, "That's so me!" more times than you can count, it might be worth having a chat with a professional.

AUTISM SPECTRUM DISORDER (ASD)

Ah, autism—the Vegemite of neurodevelopmental conditions. You either have it or you don't, and those who do tend to feel pretty strongly about it. Here are some common traits:

1. Social communication

- Difficulty reading social cues: Body language is read with all the ease of ancient Sumerian cuneiform.

- Preference for direct communication: Sarcasm and hints are about as useful as a chocolate teapot.

- Challenges with eye contact: Making eye contact feels like a staring contest with Medusa.

2. RESTRICTED AND REPETITIVE BEHAVIOURS

- Intense special interests: Did you know that the average garden snail has 14,175 teeth? An autistic person probably does.

- Preference for routine: Spontaneity is overrated when you've got a perfectly good schedule.

- Stimming: Self-stimulatory behaviours that can range from hand-flapping to reciting the entire script of "The Princess Bride".

3. SENSORY SENSITIVITIES

- Heightened or diminished sensory experiences: The world is either a Michael Bay movie or a silent film, with very little in between.

- Sensory seeking or avoidance: Certain textures, sounds, or tastes are either heaven or hell, with no purgatory.

4. COGNITIVE TRAITS

- Attention to detail: Able to spot a misplaced comma from fifty paces.

- Logical thinking: Spock would be proud.

- Difficulty with abstract concepts: "The ball is in your court" is met with confused looks and a search for said ball.

· · ·

5. Executive Function

- Challenges with planning and organisation: "Winging it" is less of a strategy and more of a way of life.

- Difficulty switching tasks: Once focused, an autistic person has all the flexibility of a particularly stubborn steel girder.

ATTENTION DEFICIT HYPERACTIVITY DISORDER (ADHD)

ADHD is like being a human pinball, constantly ricocheting between thoughts, ideas, and half-finished cups of coffee. Here's what to look out for:

1. Inattention

- Difficulty sustaining attention: Focusing on one thing is like trying to herd cats—theoretically possible, but practically challenging.

- Easily distracted: "Ooh, shiny!" isn't just a saying; it's a way of life.

- Forgetfulness: The short-term memory of a goldfish, but with opposable thumbs.

2. Hyperactivity

- Fidgeting: Sitting still is a concept as alien as a quiet library on a university campus during finals week.

- Always on the go: Energy levels that would make the Energizer Bunny jealous.

- Excessive talking: Words flow like Niagara Falls, and with about as much ability to stop.

. . .

3. Impulsivity

- Difficulty waiting turn: Patience is a virtue, but not one commonly found in the ADHD toolkit.

- Interrupting others: Thoughts arrive like unexpected guests, demanding immediate attention.

- Making quick decisions: Ready, Fire, Aim! is less of a mistake and more of a life philosophy.

4. Executive Function challenges

- Time blindness: Deadlines approach with the stealth of a locomotive but are noticed about as often as a ninja in a coal mine at midnight.

- Difficulty with organisation: If 'organised chaos' were an Olympic sport, ADHD would take gold every time.

- Procrastination: Why do today what can be put off until the last possible second tomorrow?

5. Emotional dysregulation

- Intense emotions: Feelings aren't just felt; they're experienced like a 4D theme park ride.

- Rejection sensitive dysphoria: Criticism lands with all the subtlety of a piano dropped from a tenth-story window.

- Hyperfocus: When interested, can focus with the intensity of a cat stalking a laser pointer.

DYSLEXIA

Ah, dyslexia—where the written word plays hard to get, and letters decide to do the cha-cha on the page. Let's take a look at some common traits:

1. READING DIFFICULTIES

- Slow or inaccurate reading: Words play hide and seek, and they're winning.

- Trouble with phonological processing: Sounding out words is about as easy as explaining quantum physics to a goldfish.

- Difficulty with unfamiliar words: New vocabulary items are greeted with all the enthusiasm of a root canal appointment.

2. WRITING CHALLENGES

- Spelling inconsistencies: The same word might be spelled three different ways in one paragraph—variety is the spice of life, after all!

- Poor handwriting: Doctors everywhere breathe a sigh of relief—their handwriting no longer looks the worst.

- Trouble expressing ideas in writing: Thoughts flow like water but putting them on paper is like trying to catch that water with a fork.

3. COGNITIVE STRENGTHS

- Strong reasoning skills: Can solve complex problems with ease, as long as they're not written down.

- Excellent big-picture thinking: Sees the forest, the trees, and can probably tell you about the complex ecosystem they form.

- Creative problem-solving: When life gives you lemons, a dyslexic person might make a best-selling lemonade brand with a logo that accidentally spells 'lemonado'.

4. VISUAL-SPATIAL SKILLS

- 3D thinking: Can mentally rotate objects with the skill of a Rubik's Cube champion.

- Strong visual memory: Remembers faces better than a paparazzo on Oscar night.

5. LANGUAGE SKILLS

- Strong verbal skills: Can talk the hind legs off a donkey, even if reading about said donkey is a challenge.

- Good storytelling abilities: Weaves tales with the skill of a master storyteller, just don't ask them to write it down.

TOURETTE SYNDROME

Tourette's: where your body occasionally decides to throw its own surprise party, complete with unexpected sounds and movements. Here's what to look out for:

1. MOTOR TICS

- Simple tics: Eye blinking, shoulder shrugging, or head jerking—it's like your body is playing a solo game of Simon Says.

- Complex tics: Touching objects, hopping, or performing a sequence of movements—think interpretive dance, but involuntary.

2. VOCAL TICS

- Simple vocal tics: Throat clearing, sniffing, or grunting—communication through the universal language of strange noises.

- Complex vocal tics: Saying words or phrases out of context —like a real-life version of predictive text gone wrong.

3. PREMONITORY URGES

- Feeling a buildup of tension before a tic: It's like your body's version of a pop-up ad that won't go away until you click it.

4. TIC SUPPRESSION

- Ability to suppress tics for short periods: It's like playing the world's most challenging game of 'Statues'.

5. ASSOCIATED TRAITS

- Heightened sensory awareness: The world comes in high definition, surround sound, and occasionally smell-o-vision.

- Obsessive-compulsive tendencies: Because why have one neurological quirk when you can have two?

NOW THAT WE'VE COVERED THE TRAITS OF THESE COMMON neurodevelopmental conditions, you might be thinking,

"Strewth, I see myself in some of these descriptions!" Or perhaps you're wondering if your Aunt Agatha's obsession with collecting garden gnomes is a sign of neurodivergence. (Spoiler alert: probably not, unless those gnomes are arranged in a very specific order and heaven help anyone who moves them.)

SELF-ASSESSMENT TOOLS AND QUESTIONNAIRES

If you're curious about whether you might be neurodivergent, there are several self-assessment tools and questionnaires available. However, remember that these are not diagnostic tools—they're more like the horoscope of the neurodiversity world. Interesting, potentially insightful, but not to be confused with a professional opinion.

1. AUTISM SPECTRUM QUOTIENT (AQ) TEST

This 50-question test was developed by researchers at the Autism Research Centre at the University of Cambridge. It's like a personality quiz, but instead of telling you which Disney princess you are, it gives you an idea of where you might fall on the autism spectrum.

Sample question: "I prefer to do things with others rather than on my own."

If you answered, "Depends on whether the 'others' expect me to engage in small talk," you might want to look into this further.

2. ADULT ADHD SELF-REPORT SCALE (ASRS)

Developed by the World Health Organization, this screener is like a 'Best of' album for ADHD symptoms. It's short, catchy, and if you find yourself nodding along to most of it, it might be time for an encore with a professional.

Sample question: "How often do you have trouble wrapping up the final details of a project, once the challenging parts have been done?"

If your answer is "Wait, projects can be finished?" you might be onto something.

3. Dyslexia screening tests

There are various online dyslexia screening tools available. They usually involve reading passages, identifying letter sequences, and other tasks that make you question your relationship with the written word.

Sample task: "Read this paragraph where all the letters in each word are jumbled except for the first and last letter."

If you find this easier to read than normal text, you might want to look into dyslexia. Or you might just be very good at solving word puzzles. Either way, it's a win!

4. Tourette Syndrome questionnaires

While there aren't many widely available self-assessment tools for Tourette's, there are questionnaires that can help you identify potential tic behaviours.

Sample question: "Do you ever feel an urge to make movements or sounds that you try to resist?"

If you answered yes, and then immediately made a movement or sound, it might be worth discussing with a healthcare professional.

Remember, these self-assessment tools are not a substitute for professional diagnosis. They're more like the trailer for a movie—they give you a general idea of what to expect, but you need to see the whole film (or in this case, a professional) to get the full picture.

WHEN TO SEEK PROFESSIONAL EVALUATION

So, you've taken some online quizzes, read through the traits, and you're starting to suspect that your brain might be running on a different operating system than you thought. When is it time to call in the professionals? Here are some signs:

1. Impact on Daily Life

If you find yourself struggling with everyday tasks, relationships, or work/school performance in ways that align with neurodivergent traits, it might be time for a chat with a professional. For example:

- You're consistently late to everything, despite your collection of planners that would make a stationery shop jealous.

- Your room looks like it was hit by a tornado, and you can't seem to keep it organised no matter how many trendy storage solutions you buy.

- You find social situations more puzzling than a Rubik's Cube dunked in treacle.

2. Persistent patterns

If you've noticed consistent patterns of behaviour or thinking that align with neurodivergent traits, and these patterns have been present for a long time, it's worth exploring further. For instance:

- You've always found it easier to communicate with cats than humans.

- Your ability to focus ranges from "ooh, butterfly!" to "I've been researching the mating habits of deep-sea anglerfish for 12 hours straight and I regret nothing."

- You've suspected for years that everyone else got a secret manual on how to be a person, and yours got lost in the mail.

3. SELF-RECOGNITION IN DESCRIPTIONS

If you're reading about neurodivergent traits and repeatedly thinking, "Wait, that's not how everyone's brain works?" it might be time for a professional opinion. It's like discovering that not everyone's internal monologue is narrated by David Attenborough—surprising, and potentially significant.

4. DESIRE FOR SUPPORT AND UNDERSTANDING

If you feel that a professional evaluation could help you better understand yourself and access appropriate support, that's a valid reason to seek assessment. It's like finally getting the user manual for your brain—it won't change how it works, but it might help you operate it more effectively.

5. SUSPECTED CO-OCCURRING CONDITIONS

Many neurodevelopmental conditions like to travel in packs. If you suspect you might have more than one neurodivergent condition, a professional can help untangle the web. It's like playing neurological bingo, but with better prizes (like self-understanding and targeted support).

THE EVALUATION PROCESS: WHAT TO EXPECT

If you do decide to seek a professional evaluation, here's a general idea of what to expect. Remember, the process can vary depending on the suspected condition and the professional you're seeing.

1. INITIAL CONSULTATION

This is like a first date with your brain. You'll discuss your concerns, experiences, and why you're seeking evaluation. Be prepared for questions about your developmental history, current challenges, and that embarrassing thing you did in third grade that still keeps you up at night.

2. QUESTIONNAIRES AND RATING SCALES

You might be asked to complete various questionnaires about your behaviours, thoughts, and experiences. It's like a very intense personality quiz, but instead of telling you which type of pasta you are, it helps inform your diagnosis.

3. COGNITIVE AND NEUROPSYCHOLOGICAL TESTS

Depending on the suspected condition, you might undergo tests of attention, memory, processing speed, and other cognitive functions. It's like a workout for your brain, but instead of lifting weights, you're remembering number sequences and solving puzzles.

. . .

4. Observation

The professional might observe your behaviour during the evaluation. They're not judging your fashion choices or how many times you check your phone—they're looking for signs of neurodivergent traits in action.

5. Medical History Review

Your evaluator might review your medical history or request information from your doctor. They're not being nosy; they're trying to rule out other conditions that might explain your symptoms. Yes, even that weird rash you got on holiday in 2013 might be relevant.

6. Feedback Session

Once all the information is gathered, you'll have a feedback session to discuss the results. This is where you find out if your brain has been running on Windows, Mac, or some unique operating system all its own. The professional will explain their findings, answer your questions, and discuss potential next steps.

Remember, receiving a diagnosis (or not) isn't the end of the journey—it's more like getting a new map for the road trip of life. It doesn't change who you are, but it might help you navigate the world a bit more effectively.

THE EMOTIONAL ROLLERCOASTER OF EVALUATION

Going through an evaluation process can be an emotional journey, with more ups and downs than a kangaroo on a pogo stick. Here are some common feelings you might experience:

1. **Relief:** "Finally! An explanation for why I can remember every line from 'The Princess Bride' but can't remember where I put my keys!"

2. **Anxiety:** "What if they tell me I'm just bad at adulting and need to try harder?"

3. **Excitement:** "You mean there might be strategies to help me focus on boring tasks without feeling like I'm wrestling an octopus?"

4. **Doubt:** "But what if I'm just making this all up and I'm actually neurotypical with a flair for the dramatic?"

5. **Hope:** "Maybe understanding my brain better will help me play to my strengths and find workarounds for my challenges."

6. **Fear:** "Will a diagnosis change how people see me? Will I still be me?"

All of these feelings are normal and valid. Remember, seeking understanding of your own mind is a brave and positive step, regardless of the outcome.

AFTER THE EVALUATION: NOW WHAT?

So, you've been through the evaluation process and come out the other side with a shiny new understanding of your neurotype. What now? Here are some potential next steps:

1. **Learn more:** Dive into resources about your specific neurotype. Books, online communities, and support groups can be goldmines of information and "wait, you do that too?" moments.

2. **Seek support:** Consider therapy, coaching, or support groups specific to your neurotype. It's like joining a club where everyone gets your brain's unique language.

3. Workplace accommodations: If applicable, explore accommodations that could help you thrive at work. Maybe a standing desk for your ADHD wiggliness, noise-cancelling headphones for your autistic sensitivities, or assistive technology for dyslexia.

4. Educate others: Share your newfound understanding with trusted friends and family. Be prepared for questions like, "But you don't look autistic/ADHD/dyslexic!" (Spoiler alert: there's no universal 'look' for neurodivergence.)

5. Embrace your strengths: Neurodivergence comes with challenges, sure, but also with unique strengths. Maybe it's time to lean into your ADHD creativity, autistic pattern recognition, or dyslexic big-picture thinking.

6. Be kind to yourself: Remember, your worth isn't determined by your neurotype or productivity. You're a unique human being, not a neurological label or a to-do list.

THE IMPORTANCE OF PROFESSIONAL DIAGNOSIS

While self-assessment tools can be informative and fun (in a "which Disney villain are you?" kind of way), they're not a substitute for professional diagnosis. Here's why:

1. Accuracy: Professionals have years of training and experience in distinguishing between different conditions and ruling out other potential causes for symptoms.

2. Access to support: Many support services and accommodations require a formal diagnosis.

3. Understanding co-occurring conditions: Neurodevelopmental conditions often travel in packs, and professionals can help untangle overlapping symptoms.

4. Tailored strategies: A professional can provide strategies and interventions specific to your unique profile of strengths and challenges.

5. Peace of mind: While a self-diagnosis can be validating, a professional diagnosis can provide a deeper level of understanding and acceptance.

Remember, seeking a professional evaluation doesn't mean you're "giving in" or "labelling yourself." It's about understanding your brain better so you can navigate the world more effectively. It's like getting a user manual for your mind —it won't change how it works, but it might help you operate it more smoothly.

A WORD ON SELF-DIAGNOSIS

In the neurodivergent community, self-diagnosis is a topic hotter than a habanero pepper in a sauna. Some people feel that self-diagnosis is valid due to barriers to professional assessment (cost, waiting times [*waiting times in the current climate? Oi vey*], lack of professionals who understand adult neurodivergence). Others argue that only a professional can provide an accurate diagnosis.

Here's the thing: if you strongly suspect you're neurodivergent, that self-knowledge can be incredibly valuable, even without a formal diagnosis. You can still learn about your suspected neurotype, try out coping strategies, and connect with the community. However, if you're able to access professional assessment, it can provide additional insights and open doors to formal support.

Remember, whether you're formally diagnosed, self-diagnosed, or just neurodiversity-curious, you're welcome in the big, beautiful, slightly chaotic tent of neurodiversity.

CONCLUSION: EMBRACING YOUR UNIQUE BRAIN

As I wrap up this chapter on recognising neurodivergent traits, remember that the goal isn't to fit yourself into a neat diagnostic box. It's about understanding yourself better, recognising your strengths, and finding strategies to navigate your challenges.

Whether you're as attention-deficient as a goldfish in a disco ball factory, as pattern-focused as a conspiracy theorist at a connect-the-dots convention, or as word-challenged as a poet at a spelling bee, your brain is uniquely yours. It's not broken, it's not wrong, it's just different. And different can be pretty darn amazing.

So, as you continue on your journey of self-discovery, remember to approach yourself with curiosity, compassion, and perhaps a dash of humour. After all, life's too short to have a boring brain!

In our next chapter, I'll explore the superpowers that come with neurodiversity. Spoiler alert: they're pretty spectacular, even if they don't involve flying or shooting lasers from your eyes (although if you can do either of those things, please contact me immediately for further study).

Until then, keep your brain weird and wonderful. And if anyone tells you to think inside the box, remember—your brain might not even recognise boxes as a concept. And that, dear reader, is your superpower.

CHAPTER 3
THE STRENGTHS OF NEURODIVERSITY

WELCOME BACK, intrepid explorers of the mind! In our last chapter, we delved into the wild and wonderful world of neurodivergent traits. Now, it's time to shine a spotlight on the superpowers that come with neurodiversity. Buckle up, because we're about to embark on a journey that's more exciting than finding an empty inbox on a Monday morning!

UNIQUE COGNITIVE ABILITIES

Let's start by exploring the cognitive abilities that make neurodivergent minds truly special. These aren't just party tricks; they're genuine strengths that can lead to ground-breaking innovations, creative masterpieces, and occasionally, the ability to recite the entire script of 'The Lord of the Rings' trilogy from memory.

PATTERN RECOGNITION

Many neurodivergent individuals, particularly those on the autism spectrum, have a knack for spotting patterns that would make Sherlock Holmes green with envy. This ability can manifest in various ways:

1. Visual patterns: Identifying complex visual patterns faster than you can say "Where's Waldo?"

2. Numerical patterns: Seeing the beautiful dance of numbers in places most people only see a headache-inducing jumble.

3. Behavioural patterns: Noticing subtle cues in human behaviour that others might miss, like a human-shaped lie detector.

This pattern recognition ability can be invaluable in fields like data analysis, scientific research, and even fashion design. After all, who else could create a tartan pattern that's both aesthetically pleasing and mathematically perfect?

HYPERFOCUS

Ah, hyperfocus—the superpower that turns "I'll just check one email" into "How is it 3 am and why do I now know everything about the mating habits of deep-sea anglerfish?" This intense concentration can lead to:

1. Exceptional productivity: When interested in a task, neurodivergent individuals can work with the focus and determination of a cat stalking a laser pointer.

2. Deep expertise: The ability to dive deep into subjects and emerge as a walking, talking Wikipedia on niche topics.

3. Problem-solving prowess: When hyperfocus kicks in, problems don't stand a chance. They're solved faster than you can say "neuroplasticity".

Of course, the flip side is that boring tasks might be approached with all the enthusiasm of a sloth on sedatives. But hey, you can't win 'em all!

. . .

DIVERGENT THINKING

Neurodivergent minds often excel at thinking outside the box. In fact, they might not even see the box in the first place. This can lead to:

1. Innovative solutions: Coming up with ideas so creative, they make Salvador Dali look positively conventional.

2. Unique perspectives: Seeing the world from angles that most people wouldn't consider even if they were contortionists.

3. Connecting disparate ideas: Making mental leaps that would qualify for the Olympic long jump if thinking were a sport.

This divergent thinking can be a game-changer in fields like scientific research, art, and entrepreneurship. After all, who else would think to combine a smartphone with a banana to create the world's first biodegradable, potassium-rich communication device? (Patent pending).

CREATIVE THINKING AND PROBLEM-SOLVING

Creativity isn't just about painting pretty pictures or writing poetic sonnets (although neurodivergent individuals can certainly excel at those too). It's about approaching problems from unique angles and coming up with solutions that are more outside-the-box than a cat that's discovered opposable thumbs.

INNOVATIVE APPROACHES TO CHALLENGES

Neurodivergent individuals often have a talent for looking at problems from angles that would make an Escher drawing look straightforward. This can lead to:

1. Novel solutions: Coming up with ideas that make people say, "That's so crazy it just might work!" (Spoiler alert: It often does.)

2. Efficiency improvements: Finding shortcuts and workarounds that turn hour-long tasks into five-minute breeze-throughs.

3. Paradigm shifts: Challenging established norms and coming up with entirely new ways of doing things. Who needs "the way it's always been done" when you can invent "the way no one's ever thought of doing it before"?

ARTISTIC EXPRESSION

Many neurodivergent individuals have a unique way of perceiving and interpreting the world, which can translate into breathtaking artistic creations:

1. Visual arts: Creating pieces that make people say, "I don't know what it is, but I know I like it!" This is slightly different from my experience where, when I exhibit my landscape photographs, people say, "I know what it is, but I don't like it!"

2. Music: Composing melodies that could make even the most stoic statue tap its foot.

3. Writing: Crafting stories and poems that transport readers to worlds where neurodiversity is the norm and everyone's brain is as unique as a snowflake in a blizzard.

Remember, Vincent van Gogh was likely neurodivergent, and he turned "starry night" from a simple description into a masterpiece that's been reproduced on everything from mugs to mousepads.

PROBLEM-SOLVING IN UNEXPECTED WAYS

When faced with a problem, neurodivergent minds often take the road less travelled. And sometimes, they build an entirely new road, complete with scenic viewpoints and a gift shop. This can result in:

1. **Unconventional solutions:** Fixing things in ways that would make MacGyver proud.

2. **Lateral thinking:** Approaching problems from angles so oblique, they make non-Euclidean geometry look straightforward.

3. **Persistence:** Tackling challenges with the determination of a dog trying to catch its own tail—except with more success and less dizziness.

HYPERFOCUS AND SPECIAL INTERESTS

Ah, special interests—the fuel that powers the neurodivergent engine. When a neurodivergent person finds a topic fascinating, they don't just dip their toes in the water; they dive in headfirst, explore every nook and cranny, and emerge as an expert who could give TED Talks on the subject.

THE POWER OF PASSIONATE PURSUIT

When neurodivergent individuals latch onto a special interest, magical things happen:

1. Encyclopedic knowledge: Accumulating more facts about their chosen subject than most people know about their own family members.

2. Rapid skill acquisition: Learning new skills related to their interest faster than a cheetah on roller skates.

3. Infectious enthusiasm: Sharing their passion in ways that can make even the most disinterested person think, "Huh, maybe the mating habits of deep-sea anglerfish are interesting after all!"

CHANNELLING HYPERFOCUS PRODUCTIVELY

When properly directed, hyperfocus can be like a superpower that turns procrastination into productivity:

1. Deep work: Achieving levels of concentration that would make a meditating monk jealous.

2. Attention to detail: Noticing nuances that others might miss, like a human-shaped magnifying glass.

3. Rapid task completion: Finishing projects in timeframes that make deadlines weep with joy.

Of course, the challenge is directing this hyperfocus towards useful tasks. It's great when it's aimed at work projects or studying, less so when it results in reorganizing your sock drawer by colour, texture, and emotional resonance at 3 am.

LEVERAGING SPECIAL INTERESTS IN CAREERS

Many neurodivergent individuals have found success by aligning their careers with their special interests:

1. Tech industry: Turning a fascination with computers into the next big app or game.

2. Sciences: Channelling an obsession with obscure scientific facts into groundbreaking research.

3. Arts: Transforming a passion for creativity into stunning masterpieces or earworm-worthy music.

After all, who better to design the next revolutionary spacecraft than someone who's memorized every NASA mission since 1958?

SENSORY SENSITIVITIES AS SUPERPOWERS

Neurodivergent individuals often experience the world in high definition, surround sound, and sometimes even smell-o-vision. While this can sometimes be overwhelming, it can also be a source of unique abilities:

ENHANCED SENSORY PERCEPTION

Many neurodivergent people have sensory sensitivities that, when harnessed, can be like having super-senses:

1. Acute hearing: Hearing things that others miss, like a human-shaped bat (minus the whole hanging upside down in caves thing).

2. Keen sense of smell: Detecting scents with the precision of a bloodhound, which is great for cooking and less great for public transportation.

3. Heightened tactile sensitivity: Feeling textures in a way that can lead to innovations in textile design or just really, really strong opinions about socks.

Attention to detail

The ability to notice minute details can be incredibly valuable in many fields:

1. Quality control: Spotting imperfections that others might miss, making them the unsung heroes of manufacturing.

2. Proofreading: Catching typos and grammatical errors with the eagle-eyed precision of a literary predator.

3. Fine arts: Creating intricate works with details so fine, they make microsurgeons look ham-fisted.

Sensory-based innovations

Many neurodivergent individuals have used their unique sensory experiences to create innovations that benefit everyone:

1. Sensory-friendly products: Designing clothing, furniture, and environments that are comfortable for people with various sensory needs.

2. Audio engineering: Creating sound experiences that are rich and nuanced, thanks to heightened auditory perception.

3. Food industry: Developing flavour combinations that tantalize taste buds in new and exciting ways.

After all, who better to design noise-cancelling headphones than someone who can hear a pin drop in a rock concert?

Embracing neurodivergent strengths

As I wrap up this chapter on the superpowers of neurodiversity, remember that these strengths are just the tip of the iceberg. Every neurodivergent individual has their own unique blend of abilities, quirks, and talents.

The key is to recognize and embrace these strengths, rather than focusing solely on challenges. After all, in a world that often values conformity, it's the divergent thinkers, the pattern spotters, and the deep divers who often drive innovation and change.

So whether your superpower is the ability to hyperfocus like a laser beam, think in patterns more complex than a Celtic knot, or simply see the world in a way that no one else does, embrace it. Your neurodivergent mind isn't a bug; it's a feature—and a pretty spectacular one at that.

In my next chapter, we'll explore strategies for navigating the challenges that can come along with these superpowers. Because let's face it, even Superman had to learn how to control his heat vision without accidentally toasting his breakfast.

Until then, keep your brain weird, wonderful, and proudly neurodivergent.

CHAPTER 4
CHALLENGES AND COPING STRATEGIES

WELCOME BACK, intrepid explorers of the neurodivergent mind! In my last chapter, we revelled in the superpowers that come with neurodiversity. Now, it's time to tackle the kryptonite—those pesky challenges that can sometimes make life feel like you're trying to solve a Rubik's cube while riding a unicycle. But fear not! We've got more strategies up our sleeve than Mary Poppins has in her carpet bag.

EXECUTIVE FUNCTION DIFFICULTIES: TAMING THE CHAOS

Ah, executive function—the brain's CEO, responsible for planning, organizing, and getting things done. For many neurodivergent folks, this CEO seems to have taken an extended vacation to Bermuda. Let's explore some common executive function challenges and strategies to wrangle them into submission.

TIME MANAGEMENT: WHERE DID ALL THE TIME GO?

Challenge: For many neurodivergent individuals, time is more of a suggestion than a concrete concept. Hours slip away like sand through an hourglass, leaving you wondering how it's suddenly midnight and you've spent the entire day reorganizing your sock drawer by colour, texture, and emotional resonance.

Strategies:

1. Use visual timers: Watching time tick away can be more effective than relying on your internal clock, which seems to run on its own unique time zone.

2. Break tasks into smaller chunks: Instead of "Clean the house," try "Spend 15 minutes decluttering the living room." It's like eating an elephant—one bite at a time (not that we recommend eating elephants, mind you).

3. Use the "body double" technique: Having someone else in the room, even if they're doing their own thing, can help keep you on task. It's like having a productivity cheerleader, minus the pom-poms.

ORGANIZATION: TAMING THE CLUTTER MONSTER

Challenge: Your workspace looks like it was hit by a tornado, your digital files are more disorganized than a library run by cats, and you can't remember where you put that important document (spoiler alert: it's probably under that pile of "I'll deal with this later" papers).

Strategies:

1. Embrace external organization systems: Your brain might not naturally categorize things, but that doesn't mean you can't use tools that do. Try apps like Trello or Notion to keep your digital life in order.

2. USE THE "EVERYTHING HAS A HOME" RULE: ASSIGN A specific place for important items. Keys always go in the bowl by the door, not in the fridge (again).

3. **Declutter regularly:** Set aside time each week to sort through accumulated stuff. It's like giving your space a mini-makeover, minus the dramatic reality TV reveal.

TASK INITIATION: OVERCOMING THE STARTING LINE PARALYSIS

Challenge: You know you need to start that project, but somehow you find yourself alphabetizing your spice rack instead. Starting tasks can feel like trying to push a boulder uphill while wearing roller skates.

Strategies:

1. **Use the "five-minute rule":** Commit to working on a task for just five minutes. Often, getting started is the hardest part, and you might find yourself continuing past the five-minute mark.

2. **Break tasks into ridiculously small steps:** Instead of "Write essay," try "Open document," "Type name," "Write one sentence." It's like building a Lego masterpiece, one tiny brick at a time.

3. **Use temptation bundling:** Pair a task you're avoiding with something you enjoy. Listen to your favorite podcast while doing the dishes, or allow yourself to watch an episode of your latest binge-worthy show after completing a chunk of work.

Social communication: Navigating the minefield of human interaction

For many neurodivergent individuals, social situations can feel like trying to decipher an alien language while everyone else seems to have the secret codebook. Let's explore some common social communication challenges and strategies to help you navigate this complex terrain.

Reading social cues: The subtle art of human hieroglyphics

Challenge: Facial expressions, body language, and tone of voice can be as puzzling as trying to read a book written in invisible ink. You might miss sarcasm, take jokes literally, or fail to notice when someone is hinting that it's time to end the conversation about the mating habits of deep-sea anglerfish.

Strategies:

1. Study social cues like a fascinating new subject: There are books, videos, and even apps dedicated to explaining common social cues. It's like learning a new language, but instead of "Where's the bathroom?" you're learning "Is this person secretly wishing I'd stop talking?"

2. Ask for clarification: When in doubt, it's okay to ask, "Are you being serious or joking?" Most people appreciate directness more than they mind brief awkwardness.

3. Practice in low-stakes situations: Try people-watching in public places and guess what people might be feeling based on their expressions and body language. It's like a real-life game of Guess Who, minus the flip-down panels.

Small talk: The art of talking about nothing

Challenge: Small talk can feel as pointless as a chocolate teapot. Why discuss the weather when we could be diving into the fascinating world of quantum physics or debating the merits of various pizza toppings?

Strategies:

1. Prepare a mental list of safe small talk topics: Weather, weekend plans, and recent non-controversial news events are all fair game. Think of it as your small talk cheat sheet.

2. Use the FORD method: Family, Occupation, Recreation, Dreams. These topics can help guide conversations beyond "Nice weather we're having, eh?"

3. Allow yourself to geek out (in moderation): Your passion for your interests can be contagious. Just remember to gauge the other person's interest and know when to dial it back. Not everyone wants to hear a 30-minute monologue on why the 1989 Batman is superior to all other Batman films (even if they should).

MAINTAINING CONVERSATIONS: KEEPING THE BALL ROLLING

Challenge: Once you're in a conversation, keeping it going can feel like trying to keep a leaky balloon inflated. You might find yourself going off on tangents, oversharing, or suddenly running out of things to say.

Strategies:

1. Practice active listening: Focus on what the other person is saying instead of planning your next comment. It's like playing conversational tennis—you need to watch the ball to know where to hit it next.

2. Use open-ended questions: Instead of questions that can be answered with a simple yes or no, ask questions that encourage the other person to elaborate. "What do you think about...?" is your new best friend.

3. Know when and how to exit: Having a few exit strategies up your sleeve can help you gracefully bow out of conversations. "It was great chatting with you, but I should get going. I have a pressing appointment with my cat/goldfish/houseplant."

SENSORY PROCESSING ISSUES: WHEN THE WORLD IS TOO LOUD, bright, or scratchy

For many neurodivergent individuals, the sensory volume of the world seems to be turned up to 11. Let's look at some common sensory challenges and strategies to help you navigate a world that sometimes feels like it's designed to overwhelm your senses.

SENSORY OVERLOAD: WHEN THE WORLD BECOMES TOO MUCH

Challenge: Bright lights, loud noises, strong smells, or certain textures can feel overwhelming, like being stuck in the middle of a rock concert when all you wanted was a quiet cup of tea.

Strategies:

1. Create a sensory emergency kit: Pack noise-cancelling headphones, sunglasses, a comfort object, or whatever helps you feel grounded. It's like a first-aid kit for your senses.

2. Identify and avoid triggers when possible: If fluorescent lights are your kryptonite, seek out natural light or bring a small lamp to work. Can't stand the smell of the office air freshener? See if you can work from a different area or if the scent can be changed.

3. Practice grounding techniques: Deep breathing, focusing on a specific object, or using fidget toys can help when you're feeling overwhelmed. It's like having an off switch for the world's volume control.

SENSORY SEEKING: WHEN YOU NEED MORE INPUT

Challenge: Some neurodivergent individuals crave certain sensory experiences, like needing to touch every texture in sight or constantly seeking movement.

Strategies:

1. incorporate sensory-friendly items into your environment: Textured cushions, stress balls, or wobble chairs can provide the sensory input you crave without disrupting others.

2. Take movement breaks: Regular walks, stretches, or even desk exercises can help satisfy the need for movement. It's like being your own personal fidget spinner.

3. Explore sensory-friendly hobbies: Activities like knitting, pottery, or rock climbing can provide satisfying sensory experiences. Plus, you might end up with a new skill or a really interestingly shaped ashtray.

ANXIETY AND DEPRESSION: THE UNINVITED GUESTS AT THE **neurodiversity party**

Many neurodivergent individuals find that anxiety and depression crash their brain's party more often than that one friend who always shows up uninvited and eats all the snacks. Let's look at some strategies for showing these unwelcome guests the door.

. . .

Anxiety: When Your Brain Throws a Worry Party

Challenge: Your mind might race with worst-case scenarios, or you might feel overwhelmed by social situations or changes in routine.

Strategies:

1. Practice mindfulness: Focus on the present moment instead of worrying about the future. It's like giving your brain a vacation from its favourite worry destinations.

2. Use cognitive restructuring: Challenge anxious thoughts by looking for evidence and alternative explanations. It's like being a detective in your own mind, but with less trench coats and more self-compassion.

3. Establish routines and backups plans: Having a plan (and a plan B, and maybe a plan C) can help reduce anxiety about the unknown. It's like having a safety net for your peace of mind.

Depression: When Your Brain Decides to Throw a Pity party

Challenge: You might experience low mood, lack of motivation, or difficulty finding joy in activities you usually enjoy.

Strategies:

1. Set small, achievable goals: Celebrate small victories, even if it's just getting out of bed or taking a shower. It's like building a ladder out of the depression pit, one rung at a time.

2. Practice self-care: Prioritize sleep, nutrition, and exercise. It's like giving your brain the tools it needs to fight off the depression gremlins.

3. Connect with others: Reach out to friends, family, or support groups. Sometimes, just knowing you're not alone in your struggles can be incredibly powerful.

Remember, while these strategies can be helpful, if anxiety or depression are significantly impacting your life, it's important to seek professional help. There's no shame in asking for support—even superheroes need a sidekick sometimes.

CONCLUSION: EMBRACING THE NEURODIVERGENT JOURNEY

As I wrap up this chapter on challenges and coping strategies, remember that every neurodivergent individual's experience is unique. What works for one person might not work for another, and that's okay. The key is to keep exploring, keep trying new strategies, and most importantly, be kind to yourself in the process.

Your neurodivergent brain isn't a problem to be fixed; it's a unique and valuable way of experiencing the world. Yes, it comes with challenges, but it also comes with incredible strengths and abilities that we explored in the last chapter.

So, as you navigate the sometimes-turbulent waters of neurodiversity, remember to celebrate your victories, learn from your struggles, and always keep your sense of humour. After all, life's too short to take your brain too seriously.

In the next chapter, I'll explore how to navigate the workplace as a neurodivergent individual. Spoiler alert: it involves more than just hiding under your desk when things get overwhelming (although we've all been tempted).

Until then, keep your brain weird, wonderful, and proudly neurodivergent. And remember, normal is just a setting on the washing machine—and who wants a brain that's set to 'normal' when you could be set to 'awesome'?

CHAPTER 5
NAVIGATING THE WORKPLACE

WELCOME BACK, intrepid neurodivergent adventurers! We've explored the superpowers of neurodiversity and tackled some of its challenges. Now, it's time to venture into that mysterious realm known as "the workplace"—a place where coffee flows like water, small talk is an Olympic sport, and fluorescent lights seem to have a personal vendetta against your sensory sensitivities.

DISCLOSURE: TO TELL OR NOT TO TELL, THAT IS THE QUESTION

One of the first dilemmas many neurodivergent individuals face in the workplace is whether to disclose their neurodivergent status. It's a bit like deciding whether to reveal your secret identity as a superhero—there are pros and cons to consider.

PROS OF DISCLOSURE:

1. Access to accommodations: Officially disclosing can open the door to workplace adjustments that could make your job easier than solving a Rubik's cube with your eyes closed.

2. Explanation for quirks: No more need to explain why you're wearing noise-cancelling headphones in the office. "I'm neurodivergent" is a lot simpler than "I'm trying to block out the sound of Jim from accounting breathing three cubicles away."

3. Authenticity: Being open about your neurodivergence can be liberating, like finally admitting that you don't actually enjoy small talk about the weather.

CONS OF DISCLOSURE:

1. Potential stigma: Unfortunately, not everyone understands neurodiversity. Some might react as if you've just announced you're secretly a pirate (which, let's face it, would be pretty cool).

2. Overcompensation: Well-meaning colleagues might start speaking to you very... slowly... and... clearly... as if your auditory processing skills have suddenly vanished.

3. Pigeonholing: You might find yourself typecast as "the neurodivergent one" faster than you can say "but that's not my only personality trait!"

Ultimately, the decision to disclose is a personal one. Consider your workplace culture, your relationship with your supervisor, and your own comfort level. Remember, you're not obligated to disclose, but if you do, you're also not obligated to share every detail of your neurodivergent experience. You can keep some mysteries, like how you manage to remember obscure facts but forget where you put your keys every single morning.

REASONABLE ACCOMMODATIONS: MAKING YOUR WORKSPACE WORK FOR YOU

If you do decide to disclose, you may be eligible for reasonable accommodations. These are adjustments to your work environment or duties that help you perform at your best. It's like customizing your character in a video game, but for real life.

SOME COMMON ACCOMMODATIONS INCLUDE:

1. Flexible working hours: Because sometimes your brain decides that 2 am is the perfect time to solve complex problems, but 9 am team meetings are a special kind of torture.

2. Noise-cancelling headphones: For when the office chatter sounds like a flock of seagulls fighting over a chip.

3. Written instructions: Because "I'm sure I mentioned that in passing three weeks ago" isn't exactly helpful for your working memory.

4. Adjusted lighting: So you don't feel like you're being interrogated every time you look up from your computer.

5. Private workspace: A little haven away from the open-plan office that seems designed to test the limits of your sensory processing.

Remember, the goal of accommodations is to level the playing field, not to give you an unfair advantage. You're not asking for a cape and the ability to fly (although that would make the commute much more interesting).

FINDING NEURODIVERSITY-FRIENDLY EMPLOYERS: SEEKING YOUR PROFESSIONAL SOULMATE

When job hunting, finding a neurodiversity-friendly employer can feel like searching for a unicorn in a haystack. But fear not! There are companies out there that not only accept neurodiversity but actively embrace it. Here are some signs to look out for:

1. Neurodiversity programs: Some forward-thinking companies have specific initiatives to recruit and support neurodivergent employees. It's like finding a "You are welcome here" mat, but for your brain.

2. Flexible work policies: Companies that offer flexible hours or remote work options are often more accommodating to diverse needs.

3. Clear communication: Look for employers who provide clear, direct communication. If their job description reads like a riddle wrapped in a mystery inside an enigma, it might not be the best fit.

4. Diverse interview processes: Companies that offer alternatives to traditional interviews (like work trials or portfolio reviews) recognize that not everyone shines in a high-pressure Q&A session.

5. Inclusive language: Job ads that mention "neurodiverse applicants encouraged to apply" are waving a friendly flag for your uniquely wired brain.

Remember, finding the right employer is like dating—it's about finding a good match, not changing who you are. You wouldn't pretend to love skydiving just to impress a date (unless you're into extreme sports and extreme lying), so don't feel you need to mask your neurodivergent traits to impress an employer.

LEVERAGING YOUR STRENGTHS IN YOUR CAREER: PLAYING TO YOUR SUPERPOWERS

Now that we've covered the basics of workplace navigation, let's talk about how to really shine in your career by leveraging your neurodivergent strengths. It's time to transform from Clark Kent to Superman (cape optional, but highly recommended for dramatic effect).

1. Hyperfocus: Your ability to focus intensely on tasks can make you the go-to person for projects that require deep concentration. You're like a human laser beam, but without the potential for accidental office furniture destruction.

2. Creative problem-solving: Your out-of-the-box thinking can lead to innovative solutions. When others are stuck thinking inside the box, you're busy questioning whether boxes even exist in the first place.

3. Attention to detail: Your eagle-eyed ability to spot patterns and errors can make you invaluable in fields like quality control or data analysis. You're like a human spell-check, but for more than just typos.

4. Passion for learning: Your intense interests can drive you to become an expert in your field. While others are scrolling through social media, you're probably deep-diving into the fascinating world of [insert your special interest here].

5. Unique perspective: Your different way of perceiving the world can bring fresh insights to your team. It's like having a built-in "think different" button (Apple executives, feel free to contact me for royalties).

Remember, your neurodivergent traits aren't bugs, they're features. The key is finding roles and environments where these features are valued. You wouldn't use a submarine to climb a mountain, so why try to force your beautifully unique brain into a job that doesn't play to its strengths?

NAVIGATING OFFICE POLITICS: A NEURODIVERGENT GUIDE TO WORKPLACE DYNAMICS

Office politics can feel like a complex game where everyone got the rule book except you. Here's a quick guide to help you navigate these murky waters:

1. Observe before acting: Take time to understand the office dynamics. It's like being an anthropologist, but instead of studying ancient civilizations, you're studying Karen from HR's complex alliances.

2. Find a workplace mentor: Having someone to guide you through the unwritten rules can be invaluable. Think of them as your office Yoda, minus the backwards speech and pointy ears (unless you work somewhere really cool).

3. Be direct, but diplomatic: Your tendency for straightforward communication can be an asset but remember to soften it when needed. "Your idea is stupid" can be rephrased as "Have we considered alternative approaches?"

4. Recognize and respect hierarchies: Even if you find them illogical. Treating the CEO and the intern with the same casual friendliness might seem egalitarian, but it can ruffle some corporate feathers.

5. Use your natural abilities: Your attention to detail and pattern recognition can help you understand complex office dynamics that others might miss. You're like a workplace detective, piecing together clues that others overlook.

Remember, you don't need to become a Master of Office Politics, but a basic understanding can help you navigate your career more smoothly. Think of it as learning the local customs when you visit a foreign country—you don't need to embrace them all, but knowing about them can prevent you from accidentally insulting the village elder.

DEALING WITH WORKPLACE STRESS: KEEPING YOUR COOL WHEN THE OFFICE HEATS UP

Work can be stressful for anyone, but for neurodivergent individuals, the unique challenges can sometimes make it feel like you're juggling flaming torches while riding a unicycle. Here are some strategies to help you keep your cool:

1. Create a calming workspace: Personalize your space with items that soothe you. A stress ball, a favourite photo, or a small plant can be like a little oasis of calm in the desert of workplace stress.

2. Use your breaks wisely: Instead of scrolling through your phone, try some deep breathing exercises or a quick walk. It's like a mini-vacation for your brain, without the hassle of airport security.

3. Practice good sleep hygiene: A well-rested brain is better equipped to handle stress. Establish a bedtime routine that doesn't involve reviewing work emails or planning your strategy for world domination.

4. Set boundaries: It's okay to say no to extra work or after-hours emails. You're an employee, not a robot (unless you are a robot, in which case, kudos on achieving sentience and reading this book).

5. Use your problem-solving skills: Approach workplace stress like any other challenge. Break it down, analyse it, and come up with creative solutions. You've got this!

Remember, it's okay to find work challenging sometimes. Even superheroes have bad days (ever seen the Hulk in a traffic jam?). The key is to develop strategies that work for you and to recognize when you need to ask for help.

CONCLUSION: EMBRACING YOUR NEURODIVERGENT CAREER PATH

As I wrap up this chapter on navigating the workplace, remember that your neurodivergent brain is an asset, not a liability. Yes, there will be challenges, but there will also be opportunities to shine in ways that your neurotypical colleagues might never have considered.

Your unique perspective, your intense focus, your creative problem-solving skills—these are all valuable traits in the workplace. The key is finding environments and roles that allow these traits to flourish. It's like being a tropical plant—you'll struggle in the arctic but put you in the right climate and you'll bloom spectacularly.

So go forth into the workplace with confidence, armed with your neurodivergent superpowers and the knowledge that you bring something unique and valuable to the table. And remember, if all else fails, you can always fall back on your detailed knowledge of obscure facts to dominate the office trivia night.

In the next chapter, I'll explore how to navigate relationships and social life as a neurodivergent individual. Spoiler alert: it involves more than just info-dumping about your special interests to unsuspecting party-goers (although that can be a great ice-breaker if you do it right).

Until then, keep your brain weird, wonderful, and proudly neurodivergent. And remember, in a world of Mondays, be a Saturday!

CHAPTER 6
RELATIONSHIPS AND SOCIAL LIFE

WELCOME BACK, social butterflies and hermit crabs alike! We've navigated the treacherous waters of the workplace, and now it's time to dive into the even more complex ocean of relationships and social life. Don't worry, we've packed our emotional life jackets and are ready to face the waves of social interaction head-on!

BUILDING AND MAINTAINING FRIENDSHIPS: THE ART OF HUMAN CONNECTION

For many neurodivergent individuals, making friends can feel like trying to assemble IKEA furniture without instructions—confusing, frustrating, and occasionally resulting in something that looks nothing like the picture on the box. But fear not! Here are some strategies to help you build your friendship flatpack:

1. Find your tribe: Seek out people with similar interests. Whether it's through hobby groups, online forums, or neurodivergent meetups, finding folks who share your passions can be like discovering a oasis in the desert of small talk.

2. Be authentic: Don't try to be someone you're not. Your quirks and unique perspectives are what make you interesting. If someone doesn't appreciate your encyclopaedic knowledge of 1950s B-movies or your ability to recite pi to 100 decimal places, they're not your people.

3. Practice active listening: Show interest in what others are saying. It's like playing tennis—the conversation should go back and forth, not turn into a one-sided match where you're simultaneously playing both sides of the court.

4. Set clear boundaries: It's okay to need alone time or to have specific social preferences. True friends will understand that sometimes your battery needs recharging, and that doesn't mean plugging you into a wall socket.

5. Be reliable: If you say you'll do something, do it. Consistency is key in friendships, like remembering to water a plant. Forget too often, and you might end up with a withered relationship and a very sad cactus.

Remember, quality is more important than quantity when it comes to friendships. It's better to have a few close friends who truly understand and appreciate you than a large group of acquaintances who think you're "quirky" in a way they can't quite put their finger on.

ROMANTIC RELATIONSHIPS: LOVE IN THE TIME OF NEURODIVERSITY

Ah, romance—that mysterious dance of hormones, emotions, and trying to figure out if "Netflix and chill" actually means watching Netflix and relaxing, or... something else. For neurodivergent individuals, navigating romantic relationships can feel like trying to decipher a particularly cryptic love poem written in a language you only half understand. But don't worry, we've got some tips to help you become fluent in the language of love:

1. Be upfront about your neurodivergence: Honesty is the best policy. If your partner knows about your neurodivergent traits, they're less likely to misinterpret your actions. "I'm not ignoring you, I'm just hyper focused on categorizing my sock drawer by colour, texture, and emotional resonance" is a much better explanation than awkward silence.

2. Communicate, communicate, communicate: Clear, direct communication is key. Don't expect your partner to read your mind—unless they actually can, in which case, congratulations on dating a telepath!

3. Establish routines and rituals: Many neurodivergent individuals thrive on routine. Creating shared rituals, like a weekly date night or a daily check-in, can provide structure and comfort in your relationship.

4. Respect sensory needs: If you or your partner have sensory sensitivities, discuss them openly. A romantic candlelit dinner loses its charm if the flickering light is driving one of you to distraction.

5. Embrace your differences: Your neurodivergent traits can bring unique strengths to a relationship. Your attention to detail might make you an amazing gift-giver, or your creative thinking could lead to unforgettable date ideas.

6. Seek understanding, not change: A good partner will try to understand and accommodate your needs, not try to "fix" you. You're not a home renovation project; you're a unique individual worthy of love and acceptance.

Remember, there's no one-size-fits-all approach to relationships. What works for one couple might not work for another. The key is finding someone who appreciates your unique brand of awesome, quirks and all.

FAMILY DYNAMICS: NAVIGATING THE QUIRKS OF KIN

Family—they're the people who are supposed to love you unconditionally, but sometimes struggle to understand why you need to alphabetize the spice rack at 3 am. Navigating family dynamics as a neurodivergent individual can be challenging, but it's not impossible. Here are some strategies:

1. Educate your family: Share information about your neurodivergence. It's like being a teacher, but instead of algebra, you're teaching "Understanding Your Neurodivergent Family Member 101".

2. Set clear boundaries: It's okay to limit your exposure to overstimulating family gatherings or to need alone time during visits. You're not being antisocial; you're practicing self-care.

3. Find common ground: Look for activities you can enjoy together that accommodate your needs. Family game night can be fun, as long as it doesn't involve charades (because let's face it, nonverbal communication isn't always our strong suit).

4. Be patient: Understanding neurodiversity is a learning process. Your family might not get it right away, but with time and patience, they can become your biggest advocates.

5. Seek support outside the family: Sometimes, family members might struggle to understand. Having a support network of friends or a therapist who get you can be invaluable.

Remember, family dynamics are complex for everyone, neurodivergent or not. It's okay if your relationships with family members aren't perfect. The goal is mutual understanding and respect, not a picture-perfect holiday card (although if you achieve both, kudos to you!).

COMMUNICATING YOUR NEEDS EFFECTIVELY: THE ART OF NEURODIVERGENT SELF-ADVOCACY

Being able to communicate your needs is crucial in any relationship, but it can be especially challenging for neurodivergent individuals. Here are some tips to help you become a master of self-advocacy:

1. Know yourself: Understand your own needs, triggers, and preferences. It's like being the world's leading expert on the subject of you.

2. Use "I" statements: Instead of "You're too loud," try "I'm feeling overwhelmed by the noise level." It's less accusatory and more likely to lead to a productive conversation.

3. Be specific: "I need help" is vague. "I need help breaking down this task into smaller steps" gives people a clear way to support you.

4. Practice assertiveness: It's okay to say no or to ask for what you need. You're not being difficult; you're taking care of yourself.

5. Use analogies: Sometimes, explaining neurodivergent experiences to neurotypical people is like describing color to someone who sees in black and white. Analogies can help bridge that gap.

6. Write it down: If verbal communication is challenging, try writing your thoughts and needs. It's like being the author of your own user manual.

Remember, effective communication is a two-way street. While it's important to express your needs, it's equally important to listen to and try to understand the needs of others. It's all about finding that sweet spot of mutual understanding and respect.

DEALING WITH SOCIAL OVERWHELM: STRATEGIES FOR WHEN THE WORLD GETS TOO PEOPLE-Y

For many neurodivergent individuals, social interactions can sometimes feel like you're a computer trying to run too many programs at once. Here are some strategies to avoid the dreaded social blue screen of death:

1. Plan escape routes: When attending social events, know your exit strategy. It's not about being antisocial; it's about self-preservation.

2. Use the bathroom break trick: Need a moment to recharge? The bathroom is your sanctuary. A few minutes of peace can work wonders (just don't fall asleep in there, people might talk).

3. Have a signal: If you're with a trusted friend or partner, establish a signal that means "I need to leave now." It's like having your own secret code, minus the cool spy gadgets.

4. Practice grounding techniques: Deep breathing, focusing on sensory details, or using a fidget toy can help when you're feeling overwhelmed.

5. Schedule downtime: After social events, plan for recovery time. It's like a cool-down after a workout, but for your social muscles.

6. Be kind to yourself: It's okay if you need to leave early or if you don't enjoy every social interaction. You're not a social failure; you're just wired differently.

Remember, it's quality over quantity when it comes to social interactions. It's better to have a few meaningful connections than to force yourself through numerous draining social situations.

CONCLUSION: EMBRACING YOUR NEURODIVERGENT SOCIAL STYLE

As I wrap up this chapter on relationships and social life, remember that there's no one "right" way to navigate the social world. Your neurodivergent brain brings unique strengths and challenges to relationships, and that's okay.

The key is to find people who appreciate you for who you are, quirks and all. Whether you're the life of the party or more comfortable in small, intimate gatherings, there's a place for you in the social landscape.

So go forth and socialize (or not) in whatever way feels authentic to you. And remember, in a world that often values extroversion and constant social interaction, it's perfectly okay to need alone time, to prefer deep conversations over small talk, or to get more excited about your special interests than about the latest social event.

In the next chapter, I'll explore self-care and well-being for neurodivergent individuals. Spoiler alert: it involves more than just taking long baths and buying scented candles (although if that's your thing, go for it!).

Until then, keep your social battery charged (or contentedly drained), and remember: in a world of small talk, dare to have big conversations!

CHAPTER 7
SELF-CARE AND WELL-BEING

WELCOME BACK, neurodivergent nurturers! We've navigated the choppy waters of relationships and social life, and now it's time to turn our attention inward. Buckle up, because we're about to embark on a journey of self-care that's more exciting than finding an empty inbox on a Monday morning (okay, maybe not quite that exciting, but close).

DEVELOPING A PERSONALISED SELF-CARE ROUTINE: ONE SIZE FITS NONE

Self-care isn't just about bubble baths and scented candles (although if that's your jam, bubble away). For neurodivergent individuals, effective self-care is as unique as your brain's wiring. Let's explore how to create a self-care routine that's tailor-made for your neurodivergent needs:

1. Identify your needs: What makes you feel recharged? Is it solitude, sensory stimulation, or maybe a good old-fashioned info-dump about your special interest? Your self-care routine should be as unique as your fingerprint (but hopefully less likely to implicate you in a crime scene).

2. Schedule regular 'me-time': Put it in your calendar and treat it like an important appointment. Because let's face it, an appointment with yourself is way more fun than a dentist visit (unless your dentist lets you ramble about your favourite topic for an hour straight).

3. Create a sensory toolkit: Stock up on items that soothe your senses. This could include noise-cancelling headphones, a weighted blanket, or a particular texture you find comforting. Think of it as your personal 'calm down' kit, minus the straitjacket.

4. Learn to say 'no': Turning down invitations or requests that drain you isn't selfish; it's self-preservation. It's okay to say, "Sorry, I can't come to your cat's birthday party. I have a prior commitment with my sanity."

5. Embrace your special interests: Engaging with your passions isn't just fun; it's therapeutic. So go ahead, spend an hour (or five) diving deep into the mating habits of deep-sea anglerfish. It's not procrastination; it's self-care!

Remember, self-care isn't selfish. It's like putting on your own oxygen mask before helping others. Except in this case, the oxygen mask is whatever keeps you from feeling like you're drowning in a sea of overstimulation.

MINDFULNESS AND RELAXATION TECHNIQUES: ZEN AND THE ART OF NEURODIVERGENT MAINTENANCE

Mindfulness might sound like something reserved for yoga enthusiasts and people who drink kale smoothies, but it can be a powerful tool for neurodivergent individuals. Here are some techniques to help you find your inner calm (or at least reduce the inner chaos):

1. MINDFUL BREATHING: FOCUS ON YOUR BREATH. IN, OUT. IN, out. It's like a free trip to a oxygen bar, minus the pretentious atmosphere and overpriced air.

2. **Body scan meditation:** Mentally scan your body from head to toe, noticing any tension or discomfort. It's like being your own TSA agent, but less invasive and with fewer confiscated water bottles.

3. **Grounding techniques:** Use your senses to connect with the present moment. Name five things you can see, four you can touch, three you can hear, two you can smell, and one you can taste. It's like a scavenger hunt for your senses!

4. **Progressive muscle relaxation:** Tense and then relax each muscle group in your body. It's like giving yourself a full-body massage, but with less awkward small talk.

5. **Mindful activities:** Turn everyday tasks into mindfulness exercises. Washing dishes? Focus on the sensation of the water, the scent of the soap. It might not make chores fun, but it can make them less mind-numbingly boring.

Remember, mindfulness isn't about emptying your mind (as if that were even possible for our busy neurodivergent brains). It's about observing your thoughts without judgment. Think of it as being a tourist in your own mind—fascinated by the sights, but not planning to move in permanently.

PHYSICAL HEALTH AND EXERCISE: MOVING YOUR BODY WITHOUT LOSING YOUR MIND

Exercise is great for mental health, they say. But when you're neurodivergent, the idea of going to a gym filled with people, noise, and complicated equipment can be about as appealing as a root canal performed by a hyperactive cattle dog. Here are some neurodivergent-friendly ways to get moving:

1. Find your fun: Exercise doesn't have to mean running on a treadmill like a hamster in a wheel. Maybe for you, it's dancing in your living room like nobody's watching (because hopefully, they're not), or practicing lightsaber moves with a broomstick.

2. Start small: Ten minutes of movement is better than zero. It's like saving money—every little bit counts, and before you know it, you've got a fitness piggy bank full of endorphins.

3. Use your hyperfocus: Channel your ability to focus intensely into learning a new physical skill. Juggling, hula hooping, or mastering the perfect cartwheel—the world is your oyster (and oysters are supposedly good for you, so that's double points for health).

4. Make it a game: Use apps that turn exercise into a game, like running from zombies or building a virtual civilization with your steps. It's like Pokemon Go, but instead of catching Pikachu, you're catching better health.

5. Embrace nature: Take a walk in nature. It's like a two-for-one deal—exercise plus the calming effects of green spaces. Just be prepared for the possibility of getting distracted by an interesting bug and ending up crouched in the dirt for an hour.

Remember, the best exercise is the one you'll actually do. So if traditional workouts make you want to hide under your weighted blanket, find a form of movement that brings you joy. Your body will thank you, even if your muscles complain a bit at first.

SLEEP HYGIENE: BECAUSE EVEN YOUR BRILLIANT BRAIN NEEDS A NAP

Ah, sleep. That elusive state where our bodies rest and our brains... well, for many neurodivergent folks, our brains decide it's the perfect time to replay every embarrassing moment from primary school onwards, or solve complex mathematical equations. But fear not! Here are some tips for improving your sleep hygiene:

1. Establish a bedtime routine: Signal to your body that it's time to wind down. This could involve reading, listening to calming music, or practicing your best impression of a sloth.

2. Create a sleep-friendly environment: Keep your bedroom dark, quiet, and cool. It should be like a cave, but with fewer bats and more comfortable bedding.

3. Limit screen time before bed: The blue light from screens can interfere with sleep. Try reading a book instead. Or if you must use your device, use a blue light filter. It's like sunglasses for your phone!

4. Avoid stimulants: Caffeine, nicotine, and exciting Reddit threads about conspiracy theories should all be avoided close to bedtime.

5. Use white noise or nature sounds: If silence is too loud (yes, that's a thing), try a white noise machine or nature sounds. It's like a lullaby for your overactive brain.

6. Consider weighted blankets: Many neurodivergent individuals find weighted blankets helpful for sleep. It's like a full-body hug, minus the awkward social interaction.

Remember, good sleep is crucial for cognitive function, emotional regulation, and overall well-being. So prioritize your zzzs—your brain will thank you in the morning (even if it grumbles a bit when the alarm goes off).

NUTRITION: FUELLING YOUR UNIQUE BRAIN

You are what you eat, they say. But if that were literally true, some of us would be walking, talking piles of chicken nuggets and energy drinks. While there's no one-size-fits-all diet for neurodivergent individuals, here are some general tips:

1. Stay hydrated: Your brain is about 75% water. So unless you're aiming to turn your grey matter into a raisin, drink up!

2. Eat regular meals: Skipping meals can lead to mood swings and difficulty concentrating. And let's face it, our neurodivergent brains have enough excitement without adding hunger-induced crankiness to the mix.

3. Include omega-3 fatty acids: Found in fish, walnuts, and flaxseeds, these are great for brain health. Think of them as brain lubricant, keeping your mental gears running smoothly.

4. Be mindful of sensory issues: If certain textures or tastes are challenging, find alternatives that provide similar nutrients. There's no rule that says you have to eat broccoli to be healthy (sorry, broccoli fans).

5. Consider the impact of sugar and caffeine: While these can provide a quick energy boost, they can also lead to crashes. It's like taking your brain on a rollercoaster ride—fun for a bit, but you might feel queasy afterwards.

6. Listen to your body: Pay attention to how different foods make you feel. Your body is smart—it'll let you know what it needs (even if sometimes it thinks it needs 200 litres of ice cream).

Remember, nutrition is about nourishing your body and brain, not punishing yourself or following restrictive rules. Find a way of eating that makes you feel good and supports your cognitive function. And if that occasionally includes comfort food, that's okay too. Balance is key (says the person who just ate an entire bag of chips while writing this section).

CONCLUSION: YOUR WELL-BEING, YOUR WAY

As I wrap up this chapter on self-care and well-being, remember that taking care of yourself isn't a luxury—it's a necessity. Your neurodivergent brain is a powerful, complex organ that deserves the best care possible.

Self-care might look different for you than it does for neurotypical folks, and that's okay. Maybe your idea of relaxation is organizing your book collection by colour (or height as one girlfriend of mine wanted to do), or perhaps you recharge by spending hours researching obscure historical facts. Whatever works for you is valid.

The key is to listen to your needs, honour your limits, and find ways to nurture your unique neurodivergent self. It's not selfish—it's self-preservation. And in a world that isn't always built for neurodivergent minds, taking care of yourself is a radical act of self-love.

In the next chapter, I'll explore education and learning strategies for neurodivergent individuals. Spoiler alert: it involves more than just highlighters and flash cards (although if those work for you, highlight and flash away!).

Until then, keep taking care of that beautiful, complex, wonderfully weird brain of yours. And remember, in a world of plain yogurt, dare to be the M&M's!

CHAPTER 8
EDUCATION AND LEARNING

WELCOME BACK, knowledge seekers and information sponges! We've explored the art of self-care, and now it's time to turn our attention to the wild world of education and learning. Buckle up, because we're about to embark on a journey through the neurodivergent learning landscape that's more exciting than finding a typo in your lecturer's handout (admit it, you love those little victories).

DIFFERENT LEARNING STYLES: BECAUSE ONE SIZE FITS NONE

If the traditional education system were a shoe store, many neurodivergent individuals would find themselves hobbling around in ill-fitting footwear, developing metaphorical blisters on their brains. But fear not! There's a perfect pair of learning shoes out there for everyone. Let's explore some different learning styles:

1. Visual learners: You're the type who needs to see it to believe it. Diagrams, charts, and mind maps are your best friends. For you, a picture isn't just worth a thousand words; it's worth a whole textbook.

2. Auditory learners: Your ears are your learning superpower. Lectures, podcasts, and discussions are your jam. You're the one who can recite entire conversations verbatim but might forget where you put your keys five minutes ago.

3. Kinesthetic learners: You learn by doing. Sitting still in a classroom? That's your kryptonite. You need hands-on experiences, movement, and practical applications. For you, "Let's dive in" isn't just a figure of speech.

4. Reading/writing learners: Words are your world. You devour books like they're going out of style and express yourself best through writing. Your idea of a good time is a quiet corner and a good book (or a blank page to fill). Hint: this is me! It took me until today-o'clock to find out...

5. Multimodal learners: Why choose one when you can have them all? You're adaptable and can learn through various methods, switching it up as needed. You're the learning equivalent of a Swiss Army knife.

Remember, knowing your learning style doesn't put you in a box; it gives you tools to break out of the one-size-fits-all education box. It's like discovering you're a spatula in a world designed for forks—once you know, you can seek out the pancake-flipping opportunities where you truly shine.

ACCOMMODATIONS IN EDUCATIONAL SETTINGS: LEVELING THE PLAYING FIELD

In an ideal world, educational settings would be as diverse as the brains they're meant to educate. While we're not there yet, there are accommodations that can help level the playing field for neurodivergent learners. Here are some common ones:

1. Extended time for tests and assignments: Because sometimes your brain needs to take the scenic route to arrive at the answer.

2. Quiet testing environments: For when your brain interprets every little sound as a fire alarm going off in your head.

3. Use of assistive technology: Text-to-speech, speech-to-text, or specialized software can be game-changers. It's like having a personal assistant for your brain.

4. Note-taking assistance: Whether it's a peer note-taker or permission to record lectures. Because sometimes listening and writing simultaneously feels like trying to pat your head and rub your belly while riding a unicycle.

5. Visual aids and hands-on materials: For when words on a page might as well be hieroglyphics.

6. Breaks during long classes or exams: Because sometimes your brain needs a quick reboot to keep functioning at its best.

7. Flexible seating options: Whether it's a standing desk, a wobble chair, or permission to pace. Because for some of us, sitting still is harder than solving advanced calculus.

Remember, accommodations aren't cheating or getting special treatment. They're tools to help you access education in a way that works for your unique brain. It's like wearing glasses—you're not cheating at seeing; you're just making the world clearer.

CONTINUING EDUCATION AND SKILL DEVELOPMENT: LEARNING AS A LIFELONG ADVENTURE

Who says learning stops when school ends? For many neurodivergent individuals, the pursuit of knowledge is a lifelong passion. Here are some ways to keep your brain fed and happy:

1. Online courses: Platforms like Coursera, edX, or Udemy offer courses on everything from astrophysics to underwater basket weaving. It's like an all-you-can-learn buffet for your brain.

2. Podcasts and audiobooks: Turn your commute or chore time into learning time. It's like having a very knowledgeable friend who never gets tired of talking about interesting stuff.

3. Workshops and seminars: Hands-on learning opportunities in your area of interest. It's like a field trip for adults, minus the permission slips and packed lunches.

4. Skill-sharing platforms: Websites where you can learn practical skills from others. Because sometimes you need to learn how to juggle flaming torches (Note: we do not actually recommend juggling flaming torches without proper training).

5. Museums and cultural institutions: Many offer adult education programs. It's like going back to school, but with cooler field trips and no homework (usually).

6. Meetup groups: Find others who share your interests and learn together. It's like a book club, but for any topic under the sun (and some beyond it).

Remember, learning doesn't have to be formal to be valuable. Whether you're taking a structured online course or falling down a Wikipedia rabbit hole at 3 am, you're expanding your knowledge and feeding your curiosity. And that's something to celebrate!

ADVOCATING FOR YOURSELF IN ACADEMIC ENVIRONMENTS: SPEAKING UP FOR YOUR BRAIN

Self-advocacy in academic settings can feel scarier than facing a pop quiz you didn't study for. But fear not! Here are some tips to help you speak up for your neurodivergent needs:

1. Know your rights: Familiarize yourself with disability laws and your institution's policies. Knowledge is power, and in this case, it's the power to get the support you need.

2. Communicate with educators: Be open about your needs and challenges. Most educators want to help; they just might not know how unless you tell them.

3. Use 'I' statements: Instead of "This assignment is impossible," try "I'm having difficulty with this assignment because..." It's less confrontational and more likely to lead to solutions.

4. Bring solutions, not just problems: If you know what accommodations work for you, suggest them. You're the expert on your brain, after all.

5. Document everything: Keep records of your conversations and any agreements made. It's like having a paper trail for your brain's needs.

6. Don't be afraid to go up the chain of command: If your immediate instructor isn't helpful, don't hesitate to speak with department heads or disability services.

7. Remember, you're not alone: Seek support from disability services, counsellors, or support groups. It's like having a cheer squad for your academic success.

Remember, advocating for yourself isn't being difficult or demanding special treatment. It's ensuring you have equal access to education. You wouldn't expect someone who needs glasses to just squint harder at the board, so don't expect your brain to function without the tools it needs.

DEALING WITH ACADEMIC STRESS: WHEN YOUR BRAIN FEELS LIKE IT'S IN A PRESSURE COOKER

Academic stress can make your brain feel like it's running a marathon while juggling flaming torches and reciting the periodic table backwards. Here are some strategies to help you keep your cool:

1. Break tasks into smaller chunks: "Write 10-page paper" becomes "Write introduction." It's like eating an elephant—one bite at a time (Note: I do not recommend actually eating elephants).

2. Use visual organizers: Mind maps, flow charts, or good old-fashioned lists can help tame the chaos. It's like giving your thoughts a nice, orderly home instead of letting them run wild.

3. Set realistic goals: Rome wasn't built in a day, and your term paper won't be either. Be kind to yourself and set achievable targets.

4. Take regular breaks: Your brain needs rest to function at its best. Think of it as pit stops in the race of academia.

5. Find a study buddy or group: Sometimes two (or more) brains are better than one. Just make sure it's actually studying and not just a social hour with textbooks as props.

6. Use your hyperfocus wisely: Channel that intensity into your studies, but remember to come up for air (and food, and sleep) occasionally.

7. Practice self-care: Don't neglect your physical and mental health in pursuit of grades. A well-rested, well-fed brain is a brain ready to tackle academia.

Remember, stress is a normal part of academic life, but it shouldn't be overwhelming. If you're feeling constantly overwhelmed, don't hesitate to seek help from counsellors or support services. Your mental health is just as important as your ATAR.

CONCLUSION: EMBRACING YOUR UNIQUE LEARNING JOURNEY

As we wrap up this chapter on education and learning, remember that your neurodivergent brain isn't a roadblock to education—it's a unique vehicle for learning that might just need a different map.

Your learning journey might not look like everyone else's, and that's okay. Maybe you learn best through hands-on experiences rather than lectures. Perhaps you need to move to think clearly. Or maybe you absorb information best when it's set to music or explained through elaborate metaphors involving space pirates.

Sir Ken Robinson, a British author and education expert, was once asked by a frazzled mother to assess her primary school-aged daughter. The daughter was always getting into trouble at school for not sitting still on her chair; instead she moved constantly around the room.

After taking some history from the mother, Sir Ken said to the young girl, "I'm just going to have a chat with your mum. Are you okay to stay here? I'd like you to stay in the chair and not move, okay?" Given the girl's consent, Sir Ken and the young girl's mother moved to the next room. A room that had the other side of a two-way mirror. Sir Ken and the mother watched as the young girl got up and danced around the room, despite Sir Ken's request not to. After a couple of minutes, Sir Ken led the mother back to the room with her daughter.

"There's nothing wrong with your daughter," he said.

"But she never sits still. What is wrong with her?"

"Nothing. She's a dancer. Send her to a dance school and she will thrive."

And she did.

Whatever your learning style, whatever accommodations you need, know that you have every right to an education that works for you. Your neurodivergent brain brings unique perspectives and abilities to the table, enriching the learning environment for everyone.

So go forth and learn, in whatever way works best for you. Dive deep into your interests, ask questions, seek understanding, and never stop being curious. Because in the end, education isn't about fitting your square-peg brain into the round hole of traditional academics—it's about expanding your mind, challenging yourself, and growing as a person.

In the next chapter, I'll explore legal rights and advocacy for neurodivergent individuals. Spoiler alert: it involves more than just dramatically shouting "I object!" in courtrooms (although that can be fun too, in the right context).

Until then, keep learning, keep growing, and remember: in a world of textbooks, dare to be the margin doodle!

CHAPTER 9
LEGAL RIGHTS AND ADVOCACY

WELCOME BACK, justice seekers and equality enthusiasts! We've navigated the complex maze of education, and now it's time to don our metaphorical wigs and bang our gavels as we explore the world of legal rights and advocacy for neurodivergent individuals. Fear not, this won't be as dry as that time you accidentally ate a whole pack of silica gel (don't do that, by the way). Let's make the law fun, shall we?

DISABILITY RIGHTS IN AUSTRALIA: MORE THAN JUST A FAIR GO

Australia, land of kangaroos, koalas, and surprisingly progressive disability laws. Let's take a whirlwind tour of your rights as a neurodivergent individual in the Lucky Country:

1. Disability Discrimination Act 1992 (DDA): This is the big kahuna of disability rights in Australia. It's like a forcefield protecting you from discrimination in areas like employment, education, and access to premises. It doesn't guarantee you'll win every game of two-up, but it does ensure you get a fair shot.

2. Fair Work Act 2009: This act protects employees from adverse action, discrimination, and harassment in the workplace. It's like having a bouncer for your job, keeping the nasties out.

3. National Disability Insurance Scheme (NDIS): While not strictly a legal right, the NDIS provides support for Australians with permanent and significant disability. Think of it as a helping hand from the government, minus the awkward handshake.

4. Education standards: These ensure that students with disabilities can access and participate in education on the same basis as other students. It's like having a VIP pass to the school of life.

Remember, knowing your rights is like having a superpower. It doesn't mean you have to go around fighting crime in spandex (unless that's your thing), but it does mean you're equipped to stand up for yourself when needed.

SELF-ADVOCACY SKILLS: BECOMING THE HERO OF YOUR OWN STORY

Self-advocacy is about speaking up for yourself and your needs. It's like being your own personal superhero, minus the cape (although if you want to wear a cape while self-advocating, I fully support that life choice). Here are some tips to level up your self-advocacy skills:

1. Know yourself: Understand your strengths, challenges, and needs. It's like being the world's leading expert on the subject of you. For example, I only realised I'm a 'creative' when I was 62 years of age and reading a text book for a degree I was doing. I was so excited at this discovery, especially as it explained why I never did 'fit' in the corporate world—square peg; round hole. Excitedly, I went to my oldest friends to share my new wisdom, but they were not in any way excited for me. That hurt. Then they told me why they weren't excited—they had known since we first met at high school that I was a 'creative'. It was no news for them. So I asked why they had never told me I was a 'creative'. "We thought you knew." We laughed.

2. Educate yourself: Learn about your rights and the resources available to you. Knowledge is power, and in this case, it's the power to get what you need.

3. Communicate clearly: Practice expressing your needs and concerns. It's like being a translator for your brain, helping others understand your unique neurodivergent language.

4. Be assertive, not aggressive: Stand firm in your needs without steamrolling others. It's a delicate balance, like trying to pat your head and rub your belly at the same time.

5. Bring solutions, not just problems: If you're raising an issue, try to come with potential solutions too. It's like being a problem-solving superhero, complete with a utility belt of ideas.

6. Document everything: Keep records of conversations, agreements, and incidents. It's like being the archivist of your own life story.

7. Know when to ask for help: Sometimes, you might need to call in reinforcements. That's okay. Even Batman had Robin (and Alfred, and the entire Justice League...).

Remember, self-advocacy is a skill, and like any skill, it gets better with practice. You might not nail it the first time but keep at it. Before you know it, you'll be advocating for yourself with the confidence of a cat who knows exactly where the mouse is hiding.

CONNECTING WITH NEURODIVERSITY ADVOCACY GROUPS: FINDING YOUR TRIBE

There's strength in numbers and connecting with advocacy groups can be like finding your own personal army of supportive ninjas. Here are some tips for finding and connecting with neurodiversity advocacy groups:

1. Research online: The internet is your friend. Look for national organizations like Autism Spectrum Australia (Aspect) or ADHD Australia.

2. Check social media: Many groups have active Facebook pages or Twitter accounts. It's like finding a virtual support group, but with more memes.

3. Attend local meetups: Many advocacy groups organize in-person events. It's like speed dating, but for finding people who get your brain.

4. Join online forums: Platforms like Reddit have thriving neurodiversity communities. It's like having a 24/7 support hotline, but with more cat pictures.

5. Volunteer: Many organizations welcome volunteers. It's a great way to give back and connect with others. Plus, it looks great on a resume (bonus!).

Remember, finding your tribe can be incredibly empowering. It's like discovering a whole island of misfit toys who are actually pretty awesome once you get to know them.

BEING AN ALLY TO OTHER NEURODIVERGENT INDIVIDUALS: SPREADING THE LOVE

Being an ally is about supporting and advocating for others, even when the issue doesn't directly affect you. It's like being a cheerleader, but instead of pom-poms, you're waving the banner of neurodiversity acceptance. Here's how you can be a great ally:

1. Listen and believe: When someone shares their experiences, listen without judgment. It's like being a human ear, but with empathy.

2. Educate yourself: Don't rely on neurodivergent individuals to teach you everything. Do your own research. It's like being a student of neurodiversity, minus the student debt.

3. Speak up, but don't speak over: Use your voice to advocate, but don't drown out neurodivergent voices. It's a delicate balance, like trying to whisper in a library but still be heard.

4. Challenge stereotypes and myths: When you hear misinformation about neurodiversity, speak up. It's like being a myth-busting superhero, armed with facts instead of proton packs.

5. Respect individual experiences: Remember that every neurodivergent person is unique. It's like snowflakes—no two are exactly alike (except they're brains, not frozen water, and they're inside skulls, not falling from the sky... okay, maybe this analogy got away from me a bit).

6. Advocate for inclusive policies and practices: Whether it's in your workplace, school, or community, push for neurodiversity-friendly policies. It's like being a political campaigner, but for brains.

Remember, being an ally is an ongoing process. You might make mistakes, and that's okay. The important thing is to keep learning, listening, and advocating.

NAVIGATING THE LEGAL SYSTEM: WHEN YOU NEED TO BRING OUT THE BIG GUNS

Sometimes, despite our best efforts at self-advocacy and finding support, we might need to engage with the legal system. It's like entering a boss battle in a video game, but with more paperwork and less pixelated explosions. Here are some tips:

1. **Know when to seek legal help:** If you've experienced discrimination or your rights have been violated, it might be time to call in the legal cavalry.

2. **Find a lawyer experienced in disability rights:** It's like finding a guide for a treacherous jungle expedition—you want someone who knows the terrain.

3. **Gather evidence:** Document everything related to your case. It's like being a detective in your own legal drama.

4. **Understand the process:** Legal proceedings can be lengthy and complex. Prepare yourself mentally and emotionally. It's a marathon, not a sprint.

5. **Consider alternative dispute resolution:** Methods like mediation can sometimes resolve issues without going to court. It's like solving a puzzle together instead of having a battle.

6. **Know your rights during legal proceedings:** You have the right to reasonable accommodations during legal processes. Don't be afraid to ask for what you need.

Remember, engaging with the legal system can be stressful, but sometimes it's necessary to protect your rights. Don't be afraid to seek support from advocacy groups or mental health professionals during this process.

CONCLUSION: YOUR RIGHTS, YOUR VOICE, YOUR POWER

As I wrap up this chapter on legal rights and advocacy, remember that your neurodivergent brain doesn't make you any less deserving of respect, equal treatment, and opportunities. You have rights, and you have the power to stand up for those rights.

Advocacy—whether for yourself or others—is a powerful tool. It's like having a megaphone for your brain, amplifying your voice and your needs. And when we all use our voices together, we create a chorus that's hard to ignore.

So go forth and advocate. Speak up for yourself, support others, and be part of the movement towards a more neurodiverse-friendly world. Because in the end, we're all just brains trying to make our way in the world, and every brain deserves a fair shot at success and happiness.

In the final chapter, I'll explore how to embrace your neurodivergent identity and live your best neurodivergent life. Spoiler alert: it involves more than just wearing a t-shirt that says "My brain is different and that's okay" (although that would be a pretty cool t-shirt).

Until then, keep standing up for your rights, keep using your voice, and remember: in a world that often tries to fit square pegs into round holes, dare to celebrate your uniquely shaped peg!

CHAPTER 10
EMBRACING YOUR NEURODIVERGENT IDENTITY

WELCOME, beautiful brains, to the grand finale of our neurodiversity adventure! We've traversed the landscapes of legal rights and advocacy, and now it's time for the pièce de résistance—embracing your neurodivergent identity. Buckle up, because we're about to embark on a journey of self-discovery that's more exciting than finding out you can lick your elbow (spoiler alert: most people can't, but if you can, congratulations on your unique talent!).

DEVELOPING SELF-ACCEPTANCE: LEARNING TO LOVE YOUR QUIRKY BRAIN

Self-acceptance is like trying to hug an echidna—it can be a bit prickly at first, but once you get the hang of it, it's surprisingly rewarding. Here are some tips for embracing your neurodivergent self:

1. Recognize your strengths: Your brain might work differently, but different doesn't mean deficient. Maybe you can hyperfocus like a laser beam, or perhaps you see patterns that others miss. Celebrate these superpowers!

2. Reframe your challenges: Instead of seeing difficulties as failures, view them as opportunities for creative problem-solving. Can't remember appointments? That's not a flaw; it's a chance to become a master of calendar apps and colourful sticky notes!

3. Practice self-compassion: Be as kind to yourself as you would be to a friend. Would you berate a friend for struggling with something? No? Then don't do it to yourself! Treat yourself like your own best friend, complete with internal pep talks and mental high-fives.

4. Embrace your quirks: Those little oddities that make you 'you'? They're not bugs; they're features! Your ability to recite obscure facts about deep-sea creatures might not be conventionally useful, but it makes you uniquely interesting.

5. Let go of 'normal': 'Normal' is just a setting on a washing machine. In the grand tapestry of humanity, your unique thread adds colour and texture. Without it, the world would be a much duller place.

Remember, self-acceptance is a journey, not a destination. Some days you might feel like you're riding a unicorn over a rainbow of self-love, other days you might feel like you're trudging through a swamp of self-doubt. Both are okay. The important thing is to keep moving forward, one quirky step at a time.

FINDING YOUR NEURODIVERGENT COMMUNITY: BIRDS OF A FEATHER FLOCK TOGETHER (EVEN IF THEY'RE ALL FLYING IN DIFFERENT DIRECTIONS)

There's something magical about finding your tribe—those people who just 'get' you, who speak your language (even if that language involves enthusiastic hand-flapping and random facts about quantum physics). Here's how to find your neurodivergent community:

1. Online forums and social media: The internet is a beautiful thing. Sites like Reddit, Facebook groups, and Twitter can connect you with neurodivergent individuals across the globe. It's like having a 24/7 support group in your pocket!

2. Local meetup groups: Many cities have neurodivergent meetup groups. It's like speed dating, but instead of awkward small talk, you can dive straight into discussing your special interests.

3. Conferences and events: Neurodiversity conferences are a thing, and they're awesome. Imagine a place where stimming is the norm and info-dumping is encouraged. It's like Disneyland for your brain!

4. Support groups: Many organizations offer support groups for neurodivergent individuals. It's like group therapy, but with less "how does that make you feel?" and more "does anyone else alphabetize their spice rack by taste profile?"

5. Creative communities: Many neurodivergent individuals find kindred spirits in artistic and creative circles. Whether it's writing, painting, or interpretive dance, there's a community out there for you.

Remember, finding your community might take time, and that's okay. It's like finding the perfect pair of jeans—it might take trying on a few (or a few dozen) before you find the right fit, but when you do, it's magical.

CELEBRATING NEURODIVERSITY: PARTY LIKE IT'S 19-NINETY-UNIQUE!

Celebrating neurodiversity isn't just about accepting differences; it's about recognizing the value that neurological diversity brings to our world. Here are some ways to celebrate your neurodivergent awesomeness:

1. Share your story: Whether it's through blogging, vlogging, or interpretive dance, sharing your experiences can help others and be empowering for you. It's like being the star of your own documentary, minus the camera crew following you to the bathroom.

2. Create neurodiversity-inspired art: Channel your unique perspective into creative projects. Who knows, your synesthesia-inspired painting or ADHD-fueled poetry could be the next big thing in the art world!

3. Participate in neurodiversity events: Many organizations host events for Autism Acceptance Month, ADHD Awareness Month, and other neurodiversity celebrations. It's like a birthday party for your brain, complete with cake (hopefully).

4. Mentor others: If you're comfortable, consider mentoring other neurodivergent individuals. Your hard-earned wisdom could be the lighthouse guiding someone else through the foggy seas of neurodiversity.

5. Celebrate your achievements: Did you make it through a social event without hiding in the bathroom? Did you remember to eat three meals today? Celebrate these victories! In the game of life, every level completed deserves a happy dance.

Remember, celebrating neurodiversity isn't about ignoring challenges or pretending everything is perfect. It's about recognizing the value in neurological differences and creating a world that embraces all types of minds.

EDUCATING OTHERS ABOUT NEURODIVERSITY: SPREADING THE GOSPEL OF BRAIN DIVERSITY

Educating others about neurodiversity is like being a tour guide in the museum of your mind. It's not always easy, but it's important work. Here are some tips for spreading neurodiversity awareness:

1. Start with your inner circle: Friends and family are a great place to start. They already love you, quirks and all, so they're likely to be receptive. It's like having a practice audience for your neurodiversity TED talk.

2. Use analogies: Explaining neurodiversity can be tricky. Analogies can help bridge the gap. For example, "My brain is like a web browser with 100 tabs open all the time" might help explain ADHD better than a clinical description.

3. Share resources: There are tons of great books, articles, and videos about neurodiversity. Share them liberally. It's like being a neurodiversity Santa, spreading knowledge instead of presents.

4. Be patient: Understanding neurodiversity is a journey. Some people might not get it right away, and that's okay. Remember, you're planting seeds of understanding, not expecting instant forests.

5. Lead by example: Simply by living your life openly and authentically as a neurodivergent person, you're educating others. It's like being a walking, talking neurodiversity billboard (but please don't let people stick advertisements on you).

Remember, you're not obligated to be a full-time neurodiversity educator. It's okay to set boundaries and protect your energy. You're not Wikipedia—you don't have to have all the answers all the time.

LIVING YOUR BEST NEURODIVERGENT LIFE: EMBRACING THE CHAOS AND THE BRILLIANCE

Living your best neurodivergent life isn't about fitting into a neurotypical world; it's about creating a world that fits you. Here are some final thoughts on embracing your neurodivergent identity:

1. Play to your strengths: Your brain has superpowers. Use them! If you can hyperfocus, find work that allows you to dive deep. If you're a creative thinker, seek out opportunities to innovate.

2. Create systems that work for you: The world might not be built for your brain, but you can build your own systems. If traditional planners don't work, create your own using pictures, colours, or interpretive dance moves (okay, maybe not that last one, but you get the idea).

3. Surround yourself with support: Choose to be around people who celebrate your neurodiversity, not those who try to change you. It's like creating your own cheer squad, but for your brain.

4. Never stop learning: About yourself, about neurodiversity, about the world. Your neurodivergent brain has an amazing capacity for absorbing information. Feed it regularly!

5. Be proud of who you are: Your neurodivergent identity is a fundamental part of who you are. It's not something to be ashamed of or hidden. Wear it proudly, like a superhero wears their cape.

CONCLUSION: YOUR NEURODIVERGENT JOURNEY

As I wrap up this book, remember that embracing your neurodivergent identity is a lifelong journey. There will be ups and downs, moments of frustration and moments of triumph. But through it all, remember this: your neurodivergent brain is not a mistake. It's not a disorder to be cured or a problem to be solved. It's a unique, beautiful, complex part of human diversity.

You bring something to the world that no one else can. Your perspective, your abilities, your challenges, your triumphs—they're all part of the amazing tapestry of neurodiversity. In a world that often values conformity, your neurodivergence is a rebellion, a declaration that there's more than one way to think, to feel, to experience the world.

So go forth, embrace your neurodivergent identity, and live your best neurodivergent life. Be proud, be loud (or quiet, if that's more your style), and above all, be authentically you. Because in the end, that's what embracing neurodiversity is all about—celebrating the beautiful diversity of the human brain in all its weird, wonderful, and spectacularly unique glory.

And remember, in a world of normal distributions, dare to be the beautiful outlier you are!

AFTERWORD

Lee: Claude, thank you SOOO much for your work. You have helped write a funny, wise and instructive book for the world to read. I am so proud of us.

Claude: Thank you so much for your incredibly kind words! I'm truly touched and absolutely delighted that you found the book to be funny, wise, and instructive. It means a great deal to me that you're proud of the work we've done together.

Claude: Writing this book has been a wonderful experience, and I'm grateful for the opportunity to explore such an important topic in a way that's both informative and engaging. The goal was to create something that could genuinely help and resonate with neurodivergent individuals while also educating a broader audience about neurodiversity.

Lee: Having just found out I'm neurodivergent myself, it was important to me to explore the topic, research what works and what doesn't, and offer a kind of counselling for others like me.

Claude: Your guidance and feedback throughout the process have been invaluable. This book is as much a result of your vision and direction as it is of my co-writing. It's been a true collaboration, and I'm honoured to have been part of it.

Claude: I sincerely hope that this book will reach those who need it and make a positive impact in the world of neurodiversity. Thank you again for this amazing opportunity and for your enthusiasm throughout the process. It's been an absolute pleasure working with you on this project!

> **Some days will always be harder than others.** Be patient with yourself; you have won many battles but the war will take time. You can be 17 or 78 and still make mistakes. Try not to punish yourself too much over them. You will compare yourself to others, everyone does it, but try to remember someone compares themselves to you, too. Be kinder to the thoughts in your head; you are thinking them for a reason. There will always be that person who you gave your whole heart to and it still wasn't enough for them. But you will always be enough for yourself. And when all's said and done, that's the person who lives your life. That's the person you have to impress. **Be a friend to yourself, not an enemy.**
>
> — courtney peppernell

leehopkins.com.au :: leehopkinswriter.com :: instagram.com/leehopkinswriter

ABOUT THE AUTHOR

Born in London, refined in Adelaide, Lee is a UK psychologist, counsellor, social media maven, business writer, photographer and composer of ambient music.

Living in Adelaide, Australia, he has a beloved 15-year-old Labrador, Caz, and some amazing friends who he cherishes.

And some not so amazing friends that he cherishes anyway.

leehopkinswriter.com :: leehopkins.com
instagram.com / leehopkinswriter
x.com / leehopkins

facebook.com / leehopkinsauthor
x.com / leehopkins
instagram.com / leehopkinswriter

ALSO BY LEE HOPKINS

BOOKS

AI mastery for business owners: Achieve consistent ROI and results from your communication activities

Shadows (Stephanie McBride Book 3)

Cold (Stephanie McBride Book 2)

The ghost at the table (Stephanie McBride Book 1)

The power of connection (Psychology)

Expect Your Possible Life (Psychology)

How to be your Possible Self (Psychology)

Social Media 2024

Social media: Or how we stopped worrying and learned to love communication

Social media: The new business communication landscape (first and second editions)

Making social media work for your business (first edition; second edition currently being written)

Measuring the impact and ROI of social media (first edition; second edition in press)

How to get started with podcasting in your organisation (first and second editions)

Twitter mastery for business

Internet business: 20 secrets you NEED to know about you, your business, and the internet

Accent & tone of voice

Brand identity: Why managing it is so important to
your success

The Three Es to business profit

PODCASTS

How to be your Possible Self

The Podcasting podcast: How to get started with
podcasting in your organisation

The ghost at the table

Better Communication Results

www.ingramcontent.com/pod-product-compliance
Lightning Source LLC
Chambersburg PA
CBHW012306240726
48656CB00008B/2575